# What they are saying about AMONG US

Larry Morris makes the ancient words of worship and scripture come to life through his down-to-earth stories. The well-worn words of worship that for many have lost their meaning are brought back to life in and through his narratives. His work is a gift to the church as well as to those who might be looking to make sense out of their life experiences. Larry is indeed a guide in being able to navigate the gulf that separates the church from modern culture.

Bishop B. Kirby Unti
Northwest Washington Synod, ELCA

Larry Morris's poems invite us in and create a home for us. We have a feeling that we know this story well, but Morris's keen observations invite us to take a second look. We are not disappointed by the experience.

Rev. Dr. Vernon Christopherson
Directing Pastor, Zumbro Lutheran Church
Rochester, MN

Pastor Larry Morris has completed a marvelous collection of inspiring stories and experiences that will enthrall the reader and speak to the walk of faith. His experience as a pastor who also works in the secular world as an accountant offers him special insight and perspective on faith and worship.

Rev. Michael J Anderson
Pastor, Holy Spirit Lutheran
Kirkland, WA

Larry Morris is a keen observer of life, parish life in particular. Be prepared to laugh, cry, and reflect at a deep level as you read *Among Us*. It is food for the twenty-first century's soul.

Dr. Fred Fullerton
Vice President, Spiritual and Leadership Development
Director, Wesley Center, Northwest Nazarene University
Nampa, ID

In this book, we are gently and generously invited to recognize God at work in sandwiches, stars, and combines—all the details of daily life. Larry's thoughtful, funny, and insightful voice calls out the sacred in places that surprise and delight. A book to savor.

Rev. Katy McCallum Sachse
Pastor, Holy Spirit Lutheran Church
Kirkland, WA

In this little volume of poems, Larry provides a connection between the common and the holy. Simple gestures, quiet moments, a bit of laughter, and even tears are held by words that uncover sacred places in particular moments. For those who claim faith and understand a community called church (and for those who do not), you may be surprised or find yourself nodding in agreement as our life together is hallowed in these words.

Rev. Deanna Wildermuth
Senior Pastor, Trinity Lutheran
Mercer Island, WA

What is God up to in the world? How can we participate with God in what God is doing for the sake of the world? *Among Us* overflows with poignant responses to these compelling questions. Larry's creative poems, prayers, and reflections provide a magnificent tapestry of biblical faith and spirituality woven into the fabric of daily life and the seasons of human experience.

Randy Olson, DMin, MDiv
Palliative Care Chaplain
Scottsdale, AZ

Larry Morris has compiled a thoughtful collection that explores Christian faith practices, daily living, and their sacred intersection. The reflections provide a fresh look at worship, prayer, family traditions, work, play, rest, and life's transitions, describing (and sometimes imagining) the stories of individuals who gather as the whole people of God. Some intend to give pause, rekindling a faded memory, while others are light-hearted, inviting a gentle smile.

Mark Jackson
Professor, Trinity Lutheran College
Everett, WA

# AMONG US

## STORIES OF WORSHIP AND FAITH

### LARRY P. MORRIS

BOOK PUBLISHERS NETWORK

Book Publishers Network
P.O. Box 2256
Bothell • WA • 98041
PH • 425-483-3040
www.bookpublishersnetwork.com

10 9 8 7 6 5 4 3 2 1

Printed in the United States of America

LCCN   2013947822
ISBN    978-1-937454-99-9

Editor: Julie Scandora
Cover design: Laura Zugzda
Interior design: Stephanie Martindale

Illustrations: Faith and religion © Skypixel | Dreamstime.com, Bible © Kalina Vova | Dreamstime.com, Three candles © Skyfotostock | Dreamstime.com, Way to the God © Mike_kiev | Dreamstime.com, Handy team © Dawn Hudson | Dreamstime.com, Angel with the book © Ievgen Melamud | Dreamstime.com, Prayer © Benjamin Haas | Dreamstime.com

For additional copies of this book, check at your local bookstore or on Amazon. This book is also available in multiple e-versions.

*To Eunice,*
*Mom,*
*Giver of faith*

# Contents

Among Us

# Acknowledgements

Thank you to those who have encouraged me to write and made this book possible:

Suzanne, my wife, who has watched my enjoyment of writing grow and has managed to be both honest and encouraging to me.

Spirit to Spirit: A Writer's Community for encouraging me by sharing their writing. They have often moved me and lit my own imagination, and they been a vital encouragement for me to keep at it. (You know who you are Ruth, RuthAnn, Marlene, Dave, Beverly, Minna, Otto, DyAnne, Kim, Pat, Jackie, Susan, Fisher, Rosemarie, and others.)

Pastor Michael Anderson for using some of my material in worship.

My congregation for listening when I read my writings in classes and sermons and whenever I could!

Wendell Frerichs and Bill and Anita Smith, seminary professors (and a spouse) who shared with me their rich faith and overflowing hearts.

My Facebook friends who have responded to the writings I have posted over the years.

Thank you to those who read and reread this book to give me their own wisdom and responses: Gwen Anderson, Suzanne Morris, and Rev. Deanna Wildermuth. This book is a better book because of your responses and ideas. Any mistakes you may yet find are all mine.

Thank you to Sheryn Hara of Book Publishers Network and her team: Julie Scandora, Laura Z and Stephanie Martindale. They were a delight to work with and are treasure of solid, significant professional wisdom. I'm honored to work with them all!

# Introduction

A story well told has the power to move and inspire people. I use stories in this book to move and inspire you, first, about worship. We each bring all of our own experiences and emotions with us to worship. We bring our joys and sorrows, our struggles and successes, and they add color and depth to the ancient words that guide us. The writings about worship are meant to encourage and inspire you to bring all of yourself to worship and to be fully with God.

Some of my writings are about our holy days and seasons. These writings are meant to encourage you to reflect on these sacred times for our community.

Some of my writings are just for fun. I am pretty sure God has a sense of humor, and we should too! Otherwise ... well, let's not go there! I hope these give you a chuckle!

Some of my writings are about prayer. I used to think that there was a right way to pray and many wrong ways. I do not any more. There are many ways to pray. Over the course of my life, I have prayed in many ways and found different ways helpful in different circumstances. For example, sometimes, I find times of silence to be very helpful in my prayer life. At other times, I clearly need to rant at God! I hope these writings on prayer encourage you to find a way to pray that is helpful for you today—and give you the freedom to change as your life changes.

Some of my writings are about grace, God's amazing acceptance, which inspires and shapes my life like nothing else. It pops up at times when I least expect—and I think I expect it all of the time! Still, I'm surprised!

Bottom-line, I hope these writings inspire you.

STORIES OF WORSHIP

# AMONG US

The church was full today,
and among us were
two felons, who have served time,
fourteen people who have committed adultery,
(four of whom think they are the only ones who know),
six who have stolen from their employer,
three who have lied on their résumé,
six who yelled at their kids yesterday,
five who have done illegal drugs in the last month,
sixty-four who don't trust God to provide for them
    tomorrow,
twenty-eight who lied last week
(sixteen of whom think lying last week was the right
    thing to do),
eight people who cursed last week,
twenty-four people who are addicts
(including the six who haven't admitted it yet),
forty-one people who have not yet forgiven their
    neighbor,
fifty-seven people who said mean things about someone
    else last week,
forty-nine people who have not taken care of their
    "temple,"
twenty-seven people who are afraid that something will
    overwhelm them
(really afraid),
ninety-six people who would like their neighbor's car

or their neighbor's house or job or spouse or kids,
sixty-two people who don't think they have real gifts to
    share in this world,
thirty-one people who think they are better than others,
four people who are lazy,
eleven people who share very little of what they have
    with the church
or with any other group
or with any other person,
and
nine people who think they have figured life out and
    have no interest or need to learn anything more.

The church was full today.
And we all heard the words,
"With joy, I proclaim to you that Almighty God,
rich in mercy, abundant in love, forgives you all your sin
and grants you newness of life in Jesus Christ."

And we were all born again,
again.

# IN PEACE, IN PEACE ...
## LET US PRAY TO THE LORD

On Monday morning, her daughter couldn't BELIEVE
    her blue blouse
was STILL in the dryer,
DAMP!
She complained three times to her mom
as she stomped out the door to school.
Her mom replied with words her daughter couldn't
    quite hear,
but the daughter was sure they were mean.

On Tuesday, the mother got up early to make breakfast
    for her daughter,
waffles with strawberries,
but her daughter flew out of the bathroom,
grabbed her books,
grabbed a bar,
and said she had an early band practice.
Hrumpfffff!

On Wednesday night, she got home late.
Volley ball practice had been hard.
She had a chem test tomorrow, and she wasn't ready.
She ate in three minutes and disappeared into her room
without a word.

On Friday morning,
her daughter slept through her alarm.
Her mom knocked on the door and then stuck her head
    into the room.
"Time to get up. You've got to leave in five MINUTES!"
A low guttural sound followed.
As she closed the door, the mother muttered,
"You're so lazy."
She knew she shouldn't have said it.
It wasn't true.  She didn't mean it.
But she didn't apologize. She simply left for work.

On Saturday, they both slept in.
It had been a long week.
The daughter went out with her friends
but came home early and went to bed.
The mom spent the evening in quiet,
absorbed in a book.

Sunday morning, they went to worship together
out of habit.
The pastor asked them to speak the Kyrie after her
rather than sing it.

In peace, in peace … let us pray to the Lord.
In that moment, the daughter was caught by the words.
In peace …
She reached the four inches necessary
to take her mother's hand.
The mother glanced at her daughter
and saw her looking forward with a slender smile.
They held hands and took a deep breath.
In peace, in peace …
let us pray to the Lord.

That morning
two women,
tied by birth,
wrapped in love,
living in tension,
prayed together …
in peace.

In peace, in peace …
let us pray to the Lord.

Lord have mercy.

# KYRIE ELEISON

Kyrie Eleison
Lord have mercy

Old, old words
From a distant old world
In an old dead language
On a cold page unfurled

Kyrie Eleison
Lord have mercy

Words of regret
Words of sorrow
An act of renewal
A hope for tomorrow

Kyrie Eleison
Lord have mercy

Words spoken
For thousands of years
Words cleansed
By uncountable tears

Kyrie Eleison
Lord have mercy

Words we utter
With barely a sound
Words that free us
When we are bound

Kyrie Eleison
Lord have mercy

Words to reclaim
Words to hold dear
Love to remember
Love to call near

Kyrie Eleison
Lord have mercy

# LIFT UP YOUR HEARTS

The pastor raised her arms
and encouraged her congregation.
"Lift up your hearts."

Lift up your hearts
for joy comes in the morning.

Lift up your hearts
for God so loved the world.

Lift up your hearts
for the fruits of the Spirit are love, joy, peace, patience.

Lift up your hearts
for nothing shall separate you from the love of God,
    not death nor life, not angels nor principalities nor
    things present nor things to come, not height nor
    depth.

Lift up your hearts
for love never ends.

Lift up your hearts
for God leads you beside still waters and restores your
soul.

Lift up your hearts
for the lion shall lie down with the lamb.

Lift up your hearts
for I go to prepare a place for you.

"Lift up your hearts," she spoke,
and the congregation sang out,
"We lift them to the Lord!"

# WE LIFT THEM TO THE LORD!

In the wonder of spring
When dancing comes easily
And life is light,
Lift up your hearts!

In the heat of the summer
When growth surrounds us
And the night sky is filled with wonder,
Lift up your hearts!

In the fading beauty of autumn
When the splendor points to the finish
And the leaves become brittle,
Lift up your hearts!

In the deadness of winter
When loneliness fills the air
And it is difficult to stand,
When the goal is to survive
And outlast the struggle,
Lift up your hearts!

Wherever you are,
Whether life is gleeful and silly
Or painful and long,
Lift up your hearts
To the giver of grace,
To the breath of life,
To the lover of all.
Lift up your hearts!

# LORD, TO WHOM SHALL WE GO?

We've listened to the voices.

They told us to work hard,
and we did.
We were successful and rewarded
and comfortable
and lonely.
We need something more.

We've listened to the voices.

They told us that pleasure was ours for the taking
so we took,
and it felt good till it didn't anymore,
till we just needed more without the pleasure,
and there was no end in sight.
We need something to satisfy.

We've listened to the voices.

They told us our neighbors were the enemy.
WE should have THEIR life, THEIR spouse
THEIR car, THEIR job, THEIR parents.
And our circle of friends
became smaller with each desire,
and our lives became hollow.
We need something to bring us together

They told us that if we did everything right
our world would be right
and our reward would be comfort.
Then the tragedy happened for no reason.
There was no one to blame.
Life flew out of control.
Then came the anger, then the rage
and the depression.
We need something to hold on to,
someone to bring order to the chaos.
We need peace.

We've listened to the voices.

Lord to whom shall we go?
We have listened to the voices around us,
and our lives are empty.
You have the words of eternal life.
Open our ears.
Touch our hearts.
Help us love.
We are here,
listening
for your voice.

# THE INVITATION

The words are spoken,
"The body of Christ given for you,"
and they come.

They come with youthful energy
and with old rickety hips.
They come in sneakers
and high heels.

They come in wheelchairs
and with walkers,
with effort
and with tired eyes.

They come with passion and joy,
holding hands with friends and lovers.
They come with joy and silliness,
with faith and years of service.

They come with pains and struggles,
tears and losses,
questions and doubts.

They come inspired to love and serve.
They come bored and impatient.

They come—
the young and the old,
the rich and the poor,
the unemployed and the overworked,
farmers and teachers,
homemakers and college students,

blue collars and professionals,
programmers and plumbers,
teens and toddlers.

They have come for years,
for decades,
for centuries,
and for millennia,
and they are still coming.

They come,
carried in their parents' arms,
carried by their friends' prayers,
carried by hope and love.

They come
holding out their hands
to receive the holy,
to be nourished,
to be touched,
to be loved,
and they are.

They come,
and God is there
for them,
and God is here for you.

Come.

# FOR THE SPORT OF IT!

Those of us in the church
do serious things … seriously!
We do sorrow and grief,
repentance and commitment.
At least we work at them.
We try.
We work at compassion
and justice issues.
We do service and graciousness,
patience and kindness
with honest effort.

These are good things,
and we should do them.
They are serious tasks.
These are our callings.
They are gifts of the Spirit,
and they echo God's very self
as described in our sacred texts.

But in the middle of the Bible,
in what looks like a few almost
slipped-in words,
the psalmist writes:
"God created the leviathan …
for the sport of it!"

When I hear those words,
"for the sport of it,"
I chuckle!
I giggle.
Another gift of the Spirit!

God played!
For the sport of it.
For fun.
For a lark.
For a kick.
For a good time.
For the sport of it!

(I'll bet the translators
had fun with that!)

Perhaps, on occasion,
once in the middle of the year,
we should end our worship
with the words,
"Go in peace. Play with God
for the sport of it."

Maybe God would giggle …
I would!

# DANCE TO THE MUSIC

The drama of worship was unfolding
as music lifted the spirit.

The pastor carried the bread and wine to the altar
and prepared to serve
the holy meal.

The ushers passed the offering plates
as those present shared
what they were able.

All the while,
in a back aisle,
two little girls held hands
and danced to the music,
living out their joy
to the smiles of those around them.

And the heart of God
was touched that day
by simple acts
and dancing feet.

Go in peace. Serve the Lord.
And dance to the music!

# GIVEN FOR YOU

He cupped his hands
and received the body of Christ
from the hands of a holy woman,
"Given for you."

As he returned to his seat,
the twenty-three-year-old
passed by an eighty-seven-year-old friend.
The young man put his hand
on the older man's back and smiled.
The elder friend, looking down,
quietly nodded.

In that simple moment,
in that common physical act,
the generations came together,
youth merged with age,
passion merged with wisdom,
and
love became incarnate.

The body of Christ moved from bread and wine
to friendship and grace.
The body of Christ became the hand
of a twenty-three-year-old holy man,
"Given for you."

# NO REGRETS

They married at twenty-five and
fumbled their way into children.
Their son was born first.
He was colicky and
rarely slept.
It was amazing they had a second child,
a daughter.

Their son struggled through school.
He knew others were smarter,
and he hated it.
They studied with him,
helped him with friends, and
agonized with him
in his struggles.

Their daughter was a quick study,
a natural leader, and
very popular.
She didn't understand when
friends hurt her, and
they cried with her
when boys broke her heart.

When their son finished trade school
and became a mechanic
and when their daughter
finished college and
ventured to a new city for new job,
they sort of took a breath.

They realized they had given their best years
to their children.
Their health was not what it had been,
and they definitely needed more sleep.
They had poured out their lives
in love.
They had no regrets.

So is it that hard to understand
what it means
when the words are spoken,
"Given and shed for you
for the forgiveness
of sin"?

No regrets.

# TEARS AT WORSHIP

I am becoming an old man,
and I often have tears in my eyes at worship
for I see around me the saints,
whose lives are bent from years of service and pain.
I have stood with some of them in their struggles,
and together we worship the God of grace and mystery.

I am becoming an old man,
and I often have tears in my eyes at worship
for I sit among the young leaders of the church,
leaders filled with passion and energy.
I've been where they are,
and I pray God's speed for their work.

I am becoming an old man,
and I often have tears in my eyes at worship
for I see the infants baptized
and the young children walking hand in hand
with their parents.
I see in those children the nurses who will heal
and the teachers who will lead future generations.
I see in those kids the pastor
who will read to me the Twenty-third Psalm when I am
    dying.

I am becoming an old man,
and I often have tears in my eyes at worship,
tears of awe,
tears of wonders seen
and of grace yet to come.
I often
have tears in my eyes at worship,
and I am always grateful.

# AND I TOO WILL DANCE

They sit together near the front of the church
nearly every Sunday.
They sing brightly.
They listen intently.
They pray fervently.
But during the offering, they talk and laugh.
They giggle until they have tears,
and everyone loves it.

They are the widows,
who have paid the price of grief,
who have made peace with sleeping alone,
who live modest lives,
and who still love to dance.

They have found life again.
They are silly.
They are endearing.
They touch each other,
at times holding hands
and at other times hugging,
always the hugging.

They don't know
that we envy their connections.
We long
for their natural and deep and easy friendships.
We long for that kind of love
that moves with abandon,
that acts without fear.

Someday,
I will sit near the front of the church
with them,
and I too will dance.
And, I will wonder,
"What took me so long?"

# THE GRACE THAT SURROUNDS US

The
acolyte
lit her
torch as
the worship
service was
ending and then
snuffed out
the candles.
The smoke
swirled from
the embers
and slowly
became a
part of the air
that surrounds us.

Our
worship was
finished, but
the encounter
continued to
smolder
in our hearts
and minds.
The Spirit
swirled
from the
songs, and
the Word
from the bread
and the wine,
and became
a part of the grace
that surrounds us.


Breath deep!

# BY WHAT NAME

The pastor had asked the question a thousand times
and would ask it another thousand
if he served long enough.
"By what name shall this child be baptized?"
What he could have asked was:
"By what name shall her childhood friends
      learn about trust?"
"By what name shall his friends
      think of kindness?"
"By what name shall her life partner
      experience the most intimate kind of love and
      forgiveness?"
"By what name shall his business partners
      understand integrity?"
"By what name shall those in her church
      know wisdom?"
"By what name shall his children
      come to experience acceptance?"
"By what name shall her neighbors
      recognize generosity?"
"By what name shall God
      bless the community?"
He could have asked all of those questions,
but first,
on this day,
he asked,
"By what name shall this child be baptized?"

# SO LONG AS WE BOTH SHALL LIVE ...

The beautiful young couple
stood in front of the congregation
and pledged their love
"in sickness and in health,
in good times and in bad ...
so long as we both shall live."

As the pastor blessed them,
they couldn't have known
that her work would take her on more trips than they
     had planned,
and it would strain their relationship.

As they exchanged rings,
they couldn't have anticipated the tears they would shed
over their coming infertility problems,
and they couldn't have known then the pain they would
     have
when their first "miracle child" would be miscarried.

Neither of them had any way of knowing on their
     wedding day
the trouble his heart would have
and that it would put him in a hospital in ten years
and it would put them in the position of saying a
     potentially final, quick goodbye,
in case the surgery didn't work.

"In sickness and in health,
in good times and in bad ...
so long as we both shall live."

Those older couples who came to the wedding
watched with excitement and tears.
The ceremony took them back to their own passion for
    their partner,
and they loved that,
yet they knew that life would test this beautiful young
    couple's promises.

The relationships of some of the couples in the
    congregation
had survived life's testing
so far.
Others had not.
All of them wished this couple the best.
They knew, in more experienced ways than the couple,
that this was a serious act
and a holy moment.
Smiles and tears.

"In sickness and in health,
in good times and in bad …
so long as we both shall live."

# IT'S A SHAME WE DON'T KNOW

He's eighty-three and is sitting
with his wife in church
waiting for worship to begin,
waiting and remembering.

He remembers when he was in grade school.
He was the fastest boy around
and won races to prove it.
In high school, he won the district
220-yard run,
setting a district record.

He remembers when
he served in the army.
He served for twelve months,
seeing the aftermath of combat.
He still recalls the sights and the smells.

He remembers when he married his high school
    sweetheart.
He has felt lucky ever since.
Their kids struggled
but have been blessed
with good sense and patience
and have made him a grandfather
eight times over.

He remembers his working years.
He worked for thirty-five years
building planes
and enjoyed most every minute.
He helped put together the
test model of most new planes
and is still proud of it.

Now he's eighty-three and sitting in church
waiting for worship to begin.
Most people around him
know him only as an old man
and a bit frail.

They never knew the fast young boy,
the army staff sergeant,
the graceful husband,
the caring father and doting grandfather,
or the proud airline assembler .

He sees the teenage boy
two pews ahead of him
and silently wishes him well.

He's glad to be here.
He's lived a fascinating life.
It's a shame we don't know.

# I SAW YOU IN WORSHIP

I saw you in worship.
You were looking at the words,
but you weren't singing.
Perhaps you didn't know the tune.
Perhaps you don't like to sing.
Perhaps you couldn't sing.

There have been days when I
couldn't sing at worship.
I was in grief
and needed to cry.
I was in pain
and was very afraid.
I was troubled
and had no voice.

It's difficult to be at worship
on those days.
On most days, I love to sing
and help carry the music
and help lift up the worship.
On troubled days,
the worship finds me
and holds me
and carries me.

I saw you in worship.
You were looking at the words,
but you weren't singing.
If you were having a difficult day,
I hope we carried you,
I hope God found you,
I hope you were held.
God be with you.

# MORNING GLORY

The tulips
    opened their petals to receive life
    and returned joy to their creator.
The grape hyacinths
    danced with each other
    in solemn magnificence.
The apple blossoms
    erupted with new life
    and showed signs of more grace to come.
Even the grass stood at attention,
    each blade adding its own emerald wonder
    to the verdant glow of the lawn.
All along, the robins and sparrows
    sang hymns of joy and laughter.
As I sat on the deck
    with my friends,
    the flowers and the birds,
    we all worshipped.
Such morning glory!

# WORSHIP, SWEET WORSHIP

The altar is draped in soft white cloth,
ready to host the holy meal.
The solid classic wooden pulpit
stands ready for the proclamation.
The empty cross with its colorful swirls
quietly reminds us
that death has lost its sting.
And the banner with its bold colors
and simple symbols
calls us to worship.
Finally, as the sun reaches its zenith
in the late morning,
it sends its rays through the
colors of the stained-glass skylight
to dance across the floor
in front of us.
Why shouldn't creation itself
join us in worshipping
its maker?
Worship, sweet worship.
Alleluia.

INSPIRED BY THE WORD

# THE ART OF CREATION

A canvas sits on an easel.,
Next to it,
a palette with blobs of paint
and a can of brushes waits
for the artist's vision.

A slab of granite sits on the ground
alongside the chisels and hammer
and anticipates
the sculptor's dreams.

Pieces of cloth lie across the table.
Scissors, blades, and a mat
are at the ready,
patient
for the quilter's heart.

In the beginning,
the Spirit swept over the face of the waters,
ready
for the work of God.

And the creator's
vision
and dreams
and heart
began to create ...

And here you are.

# I AM

Moses asked, "Who shall I tell them has sent me?"
God answered, "Tell them I AM has sent you."
Moses did, and we still do.

"I am the beginning and the end.
    I was here at creation,
    and all things are still made through me.
I am the good shepherd.
    I will lead you by still waters
    and restore your soul.
I am the woman who has lost a coin
    and sweeps the house over and over
    searching for you.
I am the patient Father
giving you freedom
    and waiting with a party for your return.
I am the resurrection and the life.
    I know pain and separation and death,
and I will never leave you alone in those places.
I am the Word of God incarnate, in flesh.
    I have come to be with you,
    to join you, to love you.
Because I AM,
    you are,
    forever."

# THE GOOD DANCE

The great firs dance in the wind,
swaying and touching each other.
They lean toward the other, as if holding hands,
and then bend away for just a second,
flexible and filled with life,
moving seemingly with purpose and pleasure.

The couples that walk in their shade
smile and hold hands.
They talk, leaning in and then out,
laughing and listening.
They bubble over with life,
moving with purpose and pleasure.

And God saw all that was made and said,
"It is good … it is very good!"
(Gen. 1:31)

# HAGAR'S GRIEF

They say a woman's work is never done.
Cleaning and cooking
and raising children
consume and overwhelm
days and weeks and lives.
Part of this woman's special labor,
part of her obligation,
was to be a birth-mother,
a surrogate
to her master's child.
And the child would be taken,
claimed by them
until it was no longer wanted,
until it got in the way,
until the wife of the master
gave birth to her own son.
Then the slave's child
was an awkward presence,
a sign of poor faith,
an inconvenience,
a threat.

So, the slave and her child,
the mother and her son,
had to be sent
into the desert
into the sands
to disappear.
They would vanish
so the child of promise
could thrive
and our story could live on
in hope
and in purity.

Hagar, I am sorry.

# SUFFICIENT

Sufficient.
My grace is sufficient.
It was in the sermon, somewhere.
At least it was in the lessons.
It wasn't the main point.
It wasn't a point at all,
just a word, a phrase.
But on this day, it was my word,
my phrase.

How is anything sufficient
when we don't know the future
and anything could happen?
How much is enough
when my working days are dwindling
but I might live for four more decades?

What is sufficient
when our planet is warming,
our oceans are dying,
and our food is killing us slowly?

Will anything suffice
for our children, who cannot find jobs,
for our neighbors, who've lost their homes,
for those without insurance
and in need of care?

I've brought with me to this pew
my fears,
my anxieties,
and my pain.

It bothers me,
this word, my phrase,
"My grace is sufficient."
It is as if I have lost it.
The problems have become too big,
too overwhelming.

But I am here
waiting,
hoping
to be overcome
by grace once again.
Grace
that is sufficient.

# YOU DON'T HAVE TO BE A FAILURE
# TO BE A PRODIGAL

He wrote a piece of software
that everyone needed.
Within two years, he had earned
a zillion dollars.
A giant software company then
bought him out,
and he made two zillion more.

One night as he sat
in his magnificent penthouse suite
contemplating his
wealth and celebrity,
it dawned on him what he had lost.

Years ago, he had left home
and never looked back.
It was time to look,
time to remember,
time to connect.
Tears washed down his face
as he called his dad.

Within thirty minutes,
he was on his plane flying home.
His dad hugged him
as if he had just returned
from college for the first time.

They sat around the kitchen table
with cheap cookies and
a cup of joe
simply smiling at each other.
A different kind of tears
filled his eyes.

You don't have to be a failure
to be a prodigal.

Either way,
welcome home.

# I AM A CHILD OF GOD

I AM.
    I am a child of God.
I am loved unconditionally,
totally, wholly, wonderfully.
    I am a child of God.
I belong in the family.
I belong to God.
    I am a child of God.
I can be strong without putting someone down.
I can be weak and be cared for.
    I am a child of God.
I can admit I have hurt others and apologize.
I can hear the confession of others and be forgiving.
    I am a child of God.
I can be competent and let others succeed.
I can be compassionate to my neighbors and to myself.
    I am a child of God.
I can be wise and a good listener.
I can be at peace in a troubled world.
    I am a child of God.
I AM.

# HOME AT CHRISTMAS

She had attended the downtown church as a child with
    her parents.
In junior high, she went to the church's religious
    program for kids
and professed her faith when the classes were
    completed.
But she still had questions.
Faith hadn't yet moved her
as she thought it had moved others.

In college, she visited a fundamentalist church with her
    friends.
She sort of studied Buddhism.
She had friends who were Muslim,
Mormon, atheist, and whatever.

As she pulled into the parking space
to meet her parents at the Christmas Eve candlelight
    worship,
she noticed a homeless man who had parked his grocery
    cart
and was going into the church.
Stepping out of the car,
she noticed she had serendipitously parked in a place
where a star appeared to be right over the church.
In that moment,
it occurred to her that Mary and Joseph were Jewish,
the wise men were astrologers,
and the shepherds were whatever.
She felt more at home that night at St. Luke's
than she had for years.

When her parents greeted her,
they noticed that she seemed especially moved.
The holiness of that night
filled them all.

# THE KINGDOM OF GOD

The Kingdom of God is among us.
A small blue Honda in a long line of commuters
slowed so the minivan could merge.
          This is it, among us.

The owner of a sandwich shop
told the woman who couldn't find her credit card or
    cash
that she could come back another day and pay.
He handed her the sandwich,
and she was grateful.
          This is it, among us.

A young brother and sister
played catch in the front lawn
teasing and laughing
and wasting time in the best of ways.
          This is it, among us.

      The Kingdom of God is among us.

As you are getting into your car,
a friend yells your name across the parking lot
and then shouts, "Hi," and waves crazily.
You wave back and smile.
You've been recognized and named
and loved.
                    This is it, among us.

The delicate, soft, brilliant flowers
move gracefully in the breeze and
fill your heart.
          This is it, the kingdom of God, among us.

                    The angels ask
                how we can live so long
                with our eyes so closed
                while the Kingdom of God
                is so clearly, among us.

# FOUND!

I am the prodigal.
I am the Pharisee.
I am the poor soil.
I am the lost.

In my selfishness,
in my pride,
in my thoughtlessness,
you have still sought me.

You have found me
and claimed me
and changed me
and loved me.

And when I have been remade,
when life has been renewed,
I manage to run off,
and you seek me all over again.

In fear, I look for safety.
In pride, I look for acclaim.
In thoughtlessness, I look for no one.
In love, you look for me.

When I open my eyes,
you have already found me.
In joy and grief,
with love and grace,
you have found me once more!

I am loved. I am found!

# CHRISTMAS PAIN

I'm lonely, Lord.
My friends complain about having too much to do,
too many parties to attend,
too many family expectations,
too many presents to buy,
too much to do.

I don't have parties.
My family doesn't call.
The acquaintances I do have are too busy
for me.
I feel lost.
I feel alone.

But at Christmas,
we should be busy,
shouldn't we?
We should be excited, shouldn't we?
My mom should call, shouldn't she?
I'm sad.
In bed last night, I cried.

Is it wrong to want to be seen?
It is wrong to want someone to notice me?

The lights remind me,
the trees remind me,
the malls remind me
that I am alone.

In the darkness,
in my sadness,
in my fear,
the only one I can reach out for
is you.

I feel forgotten,
but I remember you, Lord.
Do you remember me?

My eyes are closed,
but my hand is out.
Do you see me?

# PSALM—HOW LONG?

How long, O Lord,
will you let your children fight
and say hurtful things about each other
that crush the spirit and destroy the soul?
How long will you let us
be mean and petty
to those who are not strong
and to those who have already lost hope?
How long will you let us see each other as the enemy
who must be vanquished
and not as brothers and sisters
whom you love?

How long will you let us keep food
from those who work
and even then cannot pay the bill?
How long will you let us shame those
who have lost their jobs,
who have lost their homes,
and who have lost hope?
How long?

How long will you let us keep our eyes closed
to those who wash our dishes
and cut our companies' lawns
and pick our lettuce
and harvest our apples
and live among us in poverty?

Hear my confession, O God.
Hear my pain.
Send your Spirit.

Fill my heart.
Open my eyes.
Open my arms.
Cleanse me, O God.

# PSALM OF PRAISE—PSALM 933

Praise God with texts and with tweeting.
Praise God on shuttles and Segways.
Praise God on tablets and pads,
on Facebook and YouTube.
Praise God wearing plaids and t-shirts,
blue jeans or suits.
Praise God in a Lexus or a Focus,
on a bike or a bus.
Praise God with your Android,
your iPhone, your pen, or your voice.
Praise the one who is still creating you
and fills your heart with tastes and sips
of goodness and grace.
Praise the one who never lets go
when you wander and forget.
Praise God who found many before you,
who will find many after you,
and who has found you now
in these words
in this moment
and called you family, again.
Praise God!

# PSALM OF FAITH—WHEREVER

When I'm lost in my pain, Lord, you find me.
When I'm lost in my sorrow, you come.
When I'm lost in myself, you call me.
When I'm lost and in danger, please run.

Wherever I am, you are there.
Wherever I go, you will be.
Wherever I wander, come after
Till I open my eyes and see.

When I find it hard to imagine,
When it's impossible for me to believe,
I touch the cross in my pocket,
And your presence reaches out for me.

Wherever I am, you are there.
Wherever I go, you will be.
Wherever I wander, come after
Till I open my eyes and see.

When the end is close, be near me.
When the struggle is fierce, say my name.
When the weariness drains, hold me to you
For your presence and love are the same.

Wherever I am, you are there.
Wherever I go, you will be.
Wherever I wander, come after
Till I open my eyes and see.

# PSALM OF LAMENT—I WAIT

O Lord, I sit in the ashes.
I have looked for you in all the places
where we have met before,
but you are not there.
Your word is dry on my lips.
Worship is no longer a song.
Silence is empty.
Even the sunlight is cold to me.
I have no tears.
I am alone.

I will wait.
I will wait for your hand on my shoulder,
your movement in my heart,
your lightness in my breath.
I will wait for your beauty in the sunrise,
your word through a friend,
your leap in my dance.
You will come.
You always do—
in a word,
in the wind,
in your time.

Till then, I sit alone
and wait.

# PSALM OF PRAYER—HEAR MY HEART

Lord,
there are prayers that are too personal,
too deep,
too hidden
to pray.
I would feel too exposed,
too vulnerable
to pray them out loud
or even
to pray them silently.
I want to pray with my whole heart,
but sometimes it is too hard.
Listen, Lord,
beneath my words,
beneath my thoughts,
and simply hear my heart.
Someday,
I will find the words,
and we will talk.
Till then,
hear my heart, Lord,
hear my heart.

# MARY, NO LONGER YOUNG

Her eyes opened early.
She lay there
and looked at her sleeping new husband.
She was still sore and in pain.
She was tired.
She rolled over and looked at her child.
He was wrapped tight.
He slept quietly, moving only his lips.
He would be hungry soon and would need her.

One year ago, she was only a girl.
She spent her days laughing with friends
and giggling at her own betrothal.

How this year had changed her.
She became pregnant, unexpectedly.
Joseph wanted to leave her,
then took her back.
In her ninth month,
they had to make the journey here.
Now she was a mother.
She didn't feel young anymore.

She now knew life would not be
what she had anticipated as a girl.
She was sure that the surprises had only begun.

But the time for pondering was over.
The baby had begun to cry.

# I STOOD ON THE SHORE

I stood on the shore
in the early morning
as the breath of God moved across the water.
The lake rippled,
the mist rose,
the trees took a breath,
and I heard in the wind,
"It is good.
It is very good."

# JESUS AND OUR MAMAS

In the Gospel according to Luke,
Jesus sent out seventy followers
in pairs.
He told them to
eat what was put before them,
heal the sick, and
preach the good news.

The healing must have been miraculous.
The preaching likely changed lives.
The eating was simply
being a good guest.

Jesus could have told them to cast out demons
or foretell the future
or raise the dead
or speak in tongues
or feed the poor.
Those activities didn't make this list of instructions,
but eating what was put in front of you did.

Our mamas also told us to eat what was put in front of
    us.
They didn't explain why either.
Perhaps we wouldn't have listened anyway.
Contentment with what we have
or with what is put in front of us
can build in us
gratitude and graciousness.
These are complicated thoughts
for a hungry ten-year-old.

Perhaps our mamas
simply knew Jesus's words.
Perhaps Jesus knew what our mamas would want.

Either way,
eating what is put before us
or practicing contentment
is a holy calling
from Jesus and our mamas!

# THE PAUSE

I'm pausing in the doorway ...
Behind me is a familiar room
with comfortable furniture
and wonderful memories.
In front of me
is the mist of my dreams,
the call of my vision.
I'm pausing
to remember all that my past has given me—
friends and love,
struggles and successes,
security and joy.
I appreciate them all.
I'm pausing
because I feel apprehensive, fearful, exposed.
All of the best adventures begin this way.
The future is never as clear as the past.
I'm pausing
for one last prayer of hope
before I step into the vision.

# WHAT A WEEK!

We've all had that kind of week …
Too much to do.
More than one person should take on.
Perhaps a bit overcommitted …
Overextended …
And then you take it on anyway.
You start with seemingly nothing,
and then …
by the end of the week …
even you are surprised by all you have done!
Perhaps you began with a plan,
and then it all falls into place.

OK, then.
I should get started.
I can't … No … I won't put this off any longer.
Time to get off the dime and do something.
No more waiting.
Time to act!

So here's my plan:
On the first day, I will create light
Then on day two, it's on to land and water,
then grass and fruit trees and hollyhocks
and a moon and sun and animals and people.
I think six days should do it.

That doesn't sound too grandiose, does it?

# THE LOAVES AND FISHES

Perhaps …

When his disciples told him to send the people away
because they were hungry and Jesus told them
to feed the crowd, they took on the task with
reluctance. When they could find only one young
boy with five loaves and two fishes, they took them
to Jesus, as if to say, "We told you so."

Then Jesus sat down and prayed while everyone just
looked and had no idea what was going to happen.
When he was finally finished praying, he told them
to pass the food out, and they began by pulling out
one loaf and one fish.

Not knowing quite what to do with so little, they simply
gave it to someone. Then another loaf to someone
else and another and another. But the basket was
still full. They pulled out loaves and fishes, yet the
basket remained full. Others came to help, and
the work of getting good food to hungry people
distracted their amazement.

Getting food to the hungry meant getting many
involved. Finally, when all had food and were full, all
of the remnants were gathered, and there were now
twelve baskets, more than when they had started!

The disciples who had spoken up so easily to send the
people away earlier were now speechless.

A young boy standing close by pointed to all of the food
and said to his mother, "Look! Look! Look!" He had
never seen so much food in one place. His mother
leaned down, gathered him up, and whispered into
his ear, "It's a miracle."

Perhaps that is how it happened. Yes, perhaps that is
exactly how it happened.

Or maybe …

When Jesus was given the five loaves and two fishes, he sat down, closed his eyes, and began to pray, and a nearby young mother handed her five-year-old son a loaf, and he awkwardly sneaked up behind Jesus, reached around and added his loaf to the basket and, on his way back, made funny expressions and giggled a little. Then two young women who had come out from the city tiptoed up and gently added a half loaf with funny little twitters. An elderly woman with a lively smile brought a loaf and had a light chuckle. The whole hillside began to see what was happening and wanted in. A man, who had come by himself, slid in a loaf and a fish. A business woman brought a whole basket of food while trying to make no noise at all! The whole hillside almost broke out in laughter when she nearly tripped over Jesus's knee. So many people came that they had to form a line. They were all careful to put down blankets and new baskets for the food, and the size of the pile made them all want to laugh out loud, but they waited!

Finally, after hundreds had passed by and everyone was watching to see what would happen, Jesus finished his prayer and opened his eyes. He saw the huge pile of food, and his eyes got bigger than they had ever been. His jaw dropped, and he looked seriously around at the crowd. Then without warning, he started to laugh, and the whole hillside joined in. They laughed and laughed until they cried. Then they opened their eyes and looked at each other and laughed some more until they all needed to take a deep breath and wipe away their tears.

Finally, Jesus told his disciples to share the food with the crowd, and they all ate until they were full. And when they gathered the remnants, all of them, there were twelve full baskets, more than anyone thought they had at the beginning.

The young boy who had sneaked up at the beginning, looked at his mother and giggled. She hugged him and whispered, "It's a miracle."

Maybe that's how it happened. Maybe that's exactly how it happened!

Does my faith hang on either of these stories being exactly, historically, precisely true? No. Does this story inspire my faith? Definitely! It inspires me to be open to the miracles that God still does in this world. And it encourages me to share my loaves and fishes more generously than I otherwise would.

Maybe that's how Jesus wants me to live. Maybe that's exactly how Jesus wants me to live.

HOLY DAYS

# DRINK DEEPLY

The water runs over the head
and back to the font.
"I baptize you …"
In that water
and in those words,
love touches us.
The invisible becomes visible,
the intangible becomes tangible,
the universal becomes personal,
"for you."
Life is renewed.
We are born a second time.
We are recreated.

Then the water returns to its work.
It runs into the drains
and into our streams,
into our rivers
and into the lakes.
It evaporates into our clouds
and gathers into our rain.
It gives life to the plants of the field
and fish in the sea
the birds of the air
and to us.

It renews
and refreshes.
It quenches
and gives life.
It comes, and it goes
again and again.

Where has this water been
that sits in this cup in front of me?
Was it at the beginning
when God separated
the dry land from the seas?
Was it there
when Moses parted the waters?
Was it there when Jesus
was baptized?
Was it there
when I was baptized?
Now it sits here
in front of me.

The water of life
that comes again
and again
is calling me to remember
God's creation in the beginning
and God's re-creation
in me
and in you.

Drink deeply.

# FATHER IN HEAVEN, FOR JESUS'S SAKE, STIR UP IN ...

Twenty-two ninth graders stood in front of our
    congregation this morning
and confirmed their faith in Jesus.
The congregation stood with them.
Then the pastors laid hands on their heads
and prayed for each of them,
"Father in heaven, for Jesus's sake
stir up in ...
the gift of your Holy Spirit.
Confirm their faith,
guide their life,
empower their serving,
give them patience in suffering,
and bring them to eternal life."

Some of the students understood the lessons
and are eager for more.
Others of the students survived their own complaints,
kept coming, and are proud that they finished.
We are proud too!
Some still have many questions about their faith
while some don't really know if they have faith at all.
"Confirm their faith, guide their life,
empower their serving ..."

Some of them already know the experience of suffering.
The father of one died when he was a child.
Some have two homes since their parents are divorced.
One has experienced brain injury,
and others have suffered in ways unspoken.
"Give them patience in suffering
and bring them to eternal life."

I sat next to a leader of the Confirmation Program,
and as the ritual took place,
I asked him if it brought back memories.
He said, "No, I was one of the kids who didn't finish.
When I told the priest I didn't believe in God,
he said I could leave—and I did!"
God found him—later.

Today twenty-two ninth graders affirmed their faith
in a public way.
There are many others who weren't there,
who don't have faith, who feel alone,
who need direction, who need encouragement,
who need love.
"Father in heaven, for Jesus's sake,
stir up
in those who have said 'no,'
in those we have missed,
in those we have written off,
in those we don't see,
in those we haven't loved,
stir up in them
the gift of your Holy Spirit.
Confirm their faith,
guide their life,
empower their serving,
give them patience in suffering,
and bring them to eternal life.
Amen."

# ASHES TO ASHES

There are parts of me that I wouldn't miss
if they were gone.
I have been greedy.
I want more than I have, and
I use more than I need.
I have been rude,
spoken about people not present,
and said things I regret.
I will not miss these parts of me when they are gone.
Ashes to ashes,
Dust to dust.

I have had experiences
that were better than perfect,
times, usually with family or friends,
that were magical,
indescribable glimpses of beauty,
times when the veil was thin.
As much as I enjoyed those times,
I don't need to be in them always.
Their power carries me still
and gives me hope.
Ashes to ashes,
Dust to dust.

I am part of this creation,
locked in time,
gifted by love, and
held in hope.
There is a grace beyond me
that someday will call me to a home,
where tears will be no more
and pain will be a distant memory.
Till then, I live with glimpses of joy
and visions of fullness.
Enough most days.
Ashes to ashes,
Dust to dust.

# REMEMBER YOU ARE DUST

"Remember you are dust
and to dust you shall return."
Smeared and spoken.
Harsh.
Jarring.
Strange.
Odd.
Distant.

"Remember you are dust
and to dust you shall return."
My time is limited.
An end is coming.
I am not forever.

"Remember you are dust
and to dust you shall return."
Among all the possibilities,
God deemed to create me,
to make me out of the chaos,
out of the dust,
then, to call me "child"
and claim me
with promise
forever.

"Remember you are dust
and to dust you shall return."
I am dust.
I am finite.
I am loved
endlessly.
Life as gift.
Remember.

# LENT, MY SERIOUS SEASON

Lent is the serious season for me.
Time to stop,
take a deep breath,
and think.
Usually,
it hits me about the time
the ashes do,
and I remember
that in due time
my body will become
a part of this earth again.
Not a bad thing.
Just a reminder
to keep thinking and loving
while I'm here.
Lent, I guess,
calls me home.

# GOOD FRIDAY

I have been with people as they die.
I have comforted others
whose loved ones have died.
I have had people I know die
of disease, of sickness,
of old age, of suicide,
and of accidents.
Jesus was executed.
I can't imagine the pain
and the anger
and the confusion.

I understand in my head
the idea of sacrifice,
but my heart rebels against
the idea of sacrifice
by execution.
It's too gruesome.
It's torture.
It gives me shivers.
It's too confusing.

Life's limits are not set by my understanding
or by my acceptance of them.
The pain in this world
goes beyond my ability to comprehend
and beyond my ability to believe.
What saves me
is that the grace in this world
is also not limited
by my ability to comprehend
or by my ability to believe.

# HOLY SATURDAY

Holy Saturday,
the day between Good Friday and Easter,
is the silence.
After the funeral of a loved one,
before the reality of death has settled in,
there comes the silence.
We get up in the morning and put two cups on the
 counter.
Then we realize …
Before we put the second cup back,
we stand there
in silence.
We pick up the phone to call.
Then we realize …
Before we put the phone down,
we stand there
in silence.

Holy Saturday is the silence after the funeral
before life resets,
before life rights itself,
before we walk for the first time into this new life.
Holy Saturday is the silence that cannot be rushed,
only lived.

Holy Saturday is the silence.

# TIME FOR EASTER

The pastor's wife had died in January
after a long struggle with cancer.
Lent came early that year,
and the whole congregation felt its weight.

As Holy Week approached,
the pastor seemed to pick up steam.
Nothing else had changed
so the congregation
thought he was healing.
He was, healing that is,
but they didn't know his plans.

After the evening Good Friday Tenebrae service,
the congregation left in darkness and silence,
as was their tradition.
The pastor went straight to his office,
took off his vestments,
and changed into painting clothes.

He and a few conspirators
then locked the doors,
rolled out large tarps,
and began to paint the entire sanctuary.
They painted it all sky blue.
They put fans in the windows
and heaters in the aisles to dry the paint quickly.

Early Saturday afternoon,
they returned to the church
and began painting again.
They painted thousands of stars
in the blue sky.
They finished that evening
and finally stepped back to look at their masterpiece.
They would call it
The Communion of Saints Sanctuary,
and whenever someone else in the congregation died,
a new star would be added to that holy space.
It was time for Easter!

PARABLES

# THE PREACHER'S BALLET SLIPPERS

Once upon a time,
there was a little girl
who couldn't sit still for very long.
After a short time sitting,
she would simply have to stand
and then move and then dance
and then smile.

Her parents were scared
to take her to church
where people sit
for a long time.
At the first church they visited,
people glared when she moved
so she sadly sat on her hands
and thought of other things.

At the next church,
after seven looooong minutes,
she began to move slowly
to the beat of the hymn
the congregation was singing.
A grandmother sitting across the aisle smiled.

During the offering,
the little girl danced in the aisle
and smiled inside and out.
When she opened her eyes,
everyone around her was smiling at her joy.
When her parents opened their eyes,
their fear went away.

Today that little girl is all grown up,
and she is the pastor of that church,
and she preaches in ballet slippers.

# TWICE BLESSED

Once there was a church that passed the offering plates
     twice
on a non-special Sunday in the middle of October.
The plates were passed at the beginning of worship,
and people contributed as they were able.
Then they all prayed together,
listened to the Word,
and sang songs of thanks.
After they shared bread and wine,
they passed the plates again,
and those with needs could take as they wanted,
and those with neighbors in need could take for them
     too.
Some might add more money to the plates.
It was a crazy idea hatched by a young intern
who is long gone,
and they only did it once.
But each fall, the stories of that event come back to life.
There is the story of a man who had lost his job
and had the courage to take some money
to buy groceries for his family.
And the story of a junior-high boy
who simply took money because he could
and later that week bought lunch for a kid who usually
     ate alone.

And then the woman whose silent tears fell into the
     offering plate
because she was free to take, even though she didn't.
And the woman who took a dollar and put it into her
     purse
and ever since has spent all of her money as if it is a gift
     from God.
Then the family who took money for their neighbor,
added more to it, and sent her to visit her daughter in
     Montana.
Passing the offering plates twice.
It was a crazy idea. They all knew it.
It would NEVER work,
not twice.

# THE PURSE

Once there was a woman named Sal.
She lived on the streets.
She was mentally ill and very afraid.
She came to the church for worship
four random times each year.
She would always come in late and sit in the back by
    herself,
gently rocking back and forth, whispering over and
    over,
"Thank you, Jesus. Thank you, Jesus. Thank you, Jesus."
She would show up at some of the Wednesday potlucks
and get her food to-go.
At the end of the food line, she would leave a tiny note.
Each time, the words on the note read,
"love always."
The kids began to welcome her when she was willing
and to help her when they were able.

When she died and was found by a stranger,
an ambulance took her directly to the morgue.
The person who took care of her body
began by removing the big red purse that she died
    clutching.
The big purse was empty except for three things:
a small pocket cross,
the pastor's business card,
and twelve tiny notes.

The pocket cross was just like the ones
the church gave to the young people in confirmation
    class.
A young girl had given one to Sal as something to hang
    onto when she needed help.
She hung on to it for nine years.

The pastor had given Sal her business card with a phone
    number
to call if she was ever in trouble.
She called—but only once
and didn't know what to say when the pastor answered,
so she hung up.

The twelve tiny notes
all said the same thing,
"love always."
Those notes will be given out to the twelve confirmation
    students
when they complete their classes
next spring.

At thanksgiving this fall,
the congregation will use that purse
as a collection plate.
It will remind them
of their mentally ill, fearful friend Sal.
It will remind them that we are all children of God.
It will remind them that life isn't always fair.
And, it will remind them
that we all have reasons
to give thanks.

# A BEAUTIFUL PORTRAIT

If her friends had been able to see inside her soul,

> *The Lord is my shepherd.*
> *I shall not want.*

they would have seen on the walls

> *Nothing shall be able to separate us*
> *from the love of God.*

verses from Holy Scripture

> *Love never ends.*

that she had made her own

> *Be still and know*
> *that I am God.*

and words, which, over the years, had claimed her.

> *Thy will be done*
> *on earth as it is in heaven.*

They would have seen prayers

> *Lord, make me an instrument of your peace.*
> *Where there is hatred, let me sow love.*

that she had prayed over and over.

> *Create in me a clean heart, O God,*
> *and renew a right spirit within me.*

They would have seen prayers
that she had celebrated with in good times

> *I lift my eyes to the hills.*
> *From where does my help come?*

and prayers that had shared her grief in hard seasons

> *My God, my God,*
> *why have you forsaken me?*

But they DID see those words.

> *Give us this day our daily bread.*

For, over the course of years, her life had become
transparent.

*whatever is true,*
*whatever is honorable,*
*whatever is just, whatever is pure,*
*whatever is lovely, whatever is commendable,*
*if there is any excellence*
*and if there is anything worthy of praise,*
*think about these things*

She didn't say everything that came to her mind,
but her words and thoughts and actions were of one
cloth.

*Love God with all your heart*
*and soul and mind*
*and your neighbor as yourself.*
Her years echoed the wisdom of Scripture,
*just as you did it to one of the least of these*
*who are members of my family, you did it to me.*
and her life had become a beautiful portrait
of faith lived boldly.

*Pray always.*
Amen, dear friend.

*Amen.*

# SHE HAD A PROBLEM WITH WATER

As a child on a winter beach, she sat down
just as a wave came up
soaking her and her grandma!
In junior high, she tipped over her teacher's water bottle,
ruining the teacher's keyboard,
losing the lesson plan,
and getting herself sent to the principal's office.

She had a problem with water.

At sixteen,
at a pre-prom party,
she tripped over a cat
and pulled her date into the swimming pool,
tuxedo and all!
In college, she forgot to put on the parking brake,
and her car slowly rolled into a creek.

She had a problem with water!

After graduate school, she's become a pastor
who is known for her crazy laughter,
her thoughtful wisdom,
and the way she throws water all over the place
when she baptizes her people!
She gives them hope.
She touches their hearts,
and they all laugh at her stories.
And when she baptizes someone,
everyone gets wet!

No one thinks she has a problem with water anymore.
They just call her
"Pastor Splash."

# GOOFY

Once there was a woman who was goofy,
the silly, funny kind of goofy.
She brought a smile to people's lips when she came into
    a room,
and it was a good bet
that laughter was soon to follow.
It came to her naturally.

In her role as a pastor,
she had also learned to be strong and compassionate
when she gathered with people grieving
or stood with a family at a death bed
or sat with a couple in trouble.
They knew they could lean on her strength,
and her compassion made it clear
they were not alone.

Later, when she was silly again,
those whom she had helped
felt the most free to laugh,
and they laughed hard.
After the laughter,
it wasn't unusual for them to cry again,
and this time,
the tears were healing ...

# AND THE PRESENCE OF GOD FINDS THEM

Once there was a pastor
who told her people
the story of Jesus,
how on the night he was betrayed
he shared bread and wine with his disciples
and gave them himself.
Then the pastor's people came to her
for a piece of bread
and the presence of God.

People walking by on the street that day
heard the story,
came into the church,
and got in line to share in the gifts.

A man said a friend was near death,
and the man had arranged for his friend
to go to the beach that very day.
The man said his friend also needed the story of Jesus
and the presence God.

So the pastor went to the beach
and found the friend
who was glad the pastor had come.
She told the story of Jesus to a teary-eyed family
and shared the bread.
Others in the park heard the words and were touched.
When the pastor invited them to share
in the bread and the presence of God,
they lined up across the park
and water lapped at their feet.

When all were fed,
someone said her sister was at the mall
and was too afraid to go to church.
So, the pastor went to the mall.
When the sister was found,
she was overcome with surprise and love,
and her fear melted away.
As the pastor told the story and shared the bread,
many others were moved by the simple gift
and the presence of God
so they lined up through the mall,
through the department store,
through the art store, and into the food court.
The security guard stayed two extra hours that night
until all were served.

Now that pastor carries
the story of Jesus and bread with her
wherever she goes.

People find her.
And the presence of God finds them.

# I SHALL DWELL IN THE HOUSE
## OF THE LORD FOREVER

When Kristen was an infant,
her grandma took care of her some days.
At nap time, Grandma would rock her slowly back and
    forth
and would gently whisper the Twenty-third Psalm,
"The Lord is my Shepherd,
I shall not want ..."
By the time she finished,
Kristen slept.

When Kristen was five,
her parents worked evenings,
so Grandma would put her to bed at night.
Grandma would sit on the edge of the bed,
hold her hand,
and quietly say the Twenty-third Psalm,
"The Lord is my shepherd,
I shall not want.
He makes me lie down in green pastures ..."
Sometimes Grandma would stop before the end
because she thought Kristen had fallen asleep.
Kristen would then whisper
"More ... more."
Grandma would finish,
and Kristen slept.

When Kristen was a senior in college,
her mother called and told her that Grandma's cancer
    was inoperable,
that they had moved her to hospice,
and that she wouldn't live long.
Kristen flew home that day

and went immediately to see Grandma.
As she stood at the side of the bed,
Grandma's breathing was heavy, and her eyes were
    closed.
Kristen had tears and didn't quite know what to say.
Finally, she took Grandma's hand and said,
"The Lord is my shepherd,
I shall not want …"
When she got to the verse
"Even though I walk through the valley of the shadow of
    death,"
she stopped and had more tears.

When Kristen paused, Grandma whispered,
"More … more."
Kristen's mother took Grandma's other hand,
and together, the two women prayed,
"Even though I walk through the valley of the shadow of
    death,
I fear no evil
for you are with me.
Your rod and your staff—they comfort me.
You prepare a table before me
in the presence of my enemies;
you anoint my head with oil;
my cup overflows.
Surely goodness and mercy shall follow me all the days
    of my life,
and I shall dwell in the house of the Lord forever."

When they finished
all three women whispered, "Forever, forever,"
and Grandma slept.

# MARY'S DREAM

Once there was a young girl
who worked hard in school
and giggled with the other girls at lunch.
She played soccer with power
and the piano with grace.
She had fun with her friends at the church.
Together, they prayed for the sick
and sent food to the hungry.

One night, she had a dream that when she was old
people would listen to her wisdom
and be at peace when she entered the room.
She thought it was odd
and quickly forgot her dream the morning after she had
     it.

When she was a senior in high school,
it worried her that she had no idea what she might study
     in college.

One Sunday morning,
while listening to Pastor Vicki preach,
the dream came back,
and her fear went away.

# THE KNIFE SALESMAN

Once there was a man who wasn't a pastor.
He was a knife salesman in the four-state region
for twenty-eight years.

His customers liked him.
As the years went by,
he celebrated with them the birth of their children,
cried as they told him of painful divorces,
listened as they told him about cancer
and heart attacks
and children that rebelled.
When it was right,
he gave them simple wisdom.
He told a few how God gave him hope,
and because of his life,
it made sense to them,
and it gave them hope.

His briefcase became the altar
upon which he leaned to pray.
He often broke bread with troubled friends,
and to those in need, he was a healing presence.

When he died,
his family wasn't surprised
that so many strangers showed up
to honor a man
who had followed his calling
and touched their hearts.

# THE IMAGE OF GOD

She had been a pastor,
a holy woman,
for twenty-three years.
She had served three congregations
and loved them all.

People knew
that she saw in them
the image of God.
She saw it as she
worked with them,
laughed with them,
confronted them,
comforted them,
and grew old with them.

She never put them down
or made fun of them
for the things they lacked
or for the fears they carried.
She saw in everyone
the image of God,
and she called it forth
with great honor
and profound wisdom.

Her people were blessed
and changed
by her vision.

In retirement,
she has taken up
painting portraits.

In the image of God,
she paints them.
Male and female,
she paints them.

"Ohhhh," people say
as they see
her vision.

"Wow," they say
to the image of God.

"Yes," they say
to each other.
"Yes."

# COMBINE BLESSING

The combine came to a slow stop,
and the farmer's pastor climbed the ladder to the
    platform
and then stepped into the cab.
After he sat down, he pulled a couple of cold ones
out of his small cooler
and gave one to the farmer.
The farmer took a look at it and shook his head.
"You brought the cheap stuff again!"
"Only the best for you!" replied his pastor.
They both laughed,
and the harvesting began again

As the wheat was cut, they talked about the dry summer
and the approaching storm.
When the wheat is ready,
it must be cut,
or it could all be lost.
Everything else has to wait.

They talked about football and fishing,
cars and tools,
and then things got quiet.
After the silence, they got serious.
The farmer talked about his wife's cancer treatment,
his daughter's troubled marriage,
and his own sense of helplessness.
The combine came to a stop again,
in the middle of the field,
as his thick stubby fingers reached for his big red
    handkerchief.

While he wiped his eyes,
his friend, his pastor,
put a hand on his back and told him
his family valued his steady love, especially now.
After a quick prayer
the farmer slowly opened his eyes and said,
"You keep coming to visit,
and I'll never get this field done!"
They both laughed out loud.

The pastor knew that when people had a need,
they had to be found
wherever they were.
Other things could wait.

At the end of the row ,
the farmer, blessed and inspired,
watched his pastor climb down and walk away,
off to bless another troubled soul.

# JUST FOR FUN

# THE BABY JESUS GOT JACKED!

Amid the forty-six thousand holiday lights
on the well-decorated lawn,
the Baby Jesus got jacked!
I could maybe understand
if they made off with Frosty or a reindeer or a plastic
    caroler.
But who lifts the Lord God Almighty?
Who pilfers the Prince of Peace?
Who snatches the Son of Mary?
Who grabs the Good Shepherd?
Who filches the Man of Sorrows?
Who jacks the Baby Jesus?
Some burglars collect hood ornaments.
Others thieves collect street signs and hang them in
    their homes.
How do you show off your stolen "Son of Mary"
    collection?
Who's impressed by an assortment of hot baby Sons of
    God?
Can you hock the Christ?
Will a pawn shop take the Alpha and the Omega?
What kind of mark-up do you give to the Lord of Glory?
The Baby Jesus got jacked.
What's this world coming to?

Or, on the other hand,
he was left out on the lawn overnight …
He was abandoned in the cold rain!
Perhaps he ran off and is changing water into wine in
     California!
Wanted: Infant in diaper. Goes by the names
Jesus, Emmanuel, and Savior.
May use the last name Josephson.
Is older than he looks, walks on water,
teaches old men, and his friends don't need health care.

Or on the third hand,
Maybe the plastic rapture happened!
Girls, count your dolls!

# HOW ARE YOU, GOD?

"How are you, God?" I prayed.
I prayed it one night when I was alone.
I didn't pray in confusion like, "WHERE are you, God?"
I didn't pray in anger as in, "WHY do I feel so alone?"
I simply prayed, "How are you, God?"
because I wanted to engage.
Then I sat back in silence.
After a moment, I smiled.
Then I chuckled at my own boldness.
I chuckled at my familiarity
with the divine.
Finally, I laughed out loud.
I had my answer.
God was fine,
and I was feeling better too—engaged!
Amen!

# MARY'S DIARY: DECEMBER 26, 0000

Dear Diary,
I felt bad last night,
chasing the angels off,
but it was late,
I was tired,
and the baby needs a schedule!
That time of night, I DON'T CARE WHO sent you!

The shepherds finally left.
They had been quiet
and stayed out of the way mostly,
just watching.
They seemed nice,
but it was a little creepy.
Dirty guys from the field …
standing around,
doing nothing but …
watching.
Seemed weird to me.

I don't know how many nights
Joseph paid to stay in this stable.
I hope not many.
I think this hay has bugs.

Joseph is talking about another dream
and needing to take us to Egypt.
I don't think he's been drinking,
but come on … Egypt?
Hey, Joe,
remember what they did
last time our people went in that direction?
Think "pyramids"!

Getting here was no fun,
pregnant and all.
Now he wants to move along and in a hurry!
He's got a lot to learn about
traveling with kids!

I can't wait to get home
and sleep on my own dirt.

My mom will want to see the baby.
Old people love babies.
Her birthday is coming next month!
She'll be thirty!

# HOW COULD I SAY NO?

I asked you, a parishioner of mine,
to do a simple task at the church.
You smiled and said, "How could I say no?"

I smiled and then thought,
"You could say no like the hundreds of others
who have said no before you."
It seemed simple for them.
They said, " No, I can't" or
"You must know someone who could do it better than I
    can" or
"No, I would be embarrassed" or
"Let me think about it"
(often meaning, "Don't make me speak the word no") or
"I'm too busy" or
"Not this time" or
"No, I haven't done that in years" or
"No, but thanks for thinking of me" or
"No, I have something else going on" or
any of a million other reasons.

But you said, "How could I say no?"
I didn't even ask in my strong voice or
my pleading voice.
I didn't grab you by the arm or threaten any kind of
    violence.
I didn't intimidate or scream or shout.
I didn't threaten to curse
or damn you
(not that I even could damn you if I wanted to, but don't
    tell anyone).
I didn't even play the guilt or the shame cards.
I probably would have forgotten the whole thing
if you had merely said, "No."

I simply asked,
and you replied, "How could I say no?"
So I answered, "Of course, you couldn't.
Thanks for volunteering!"

# THE SNAKE APP

Sssssssay there, buddy,
howssssss it hanging?
Oh me? I'm sssssssuper!
Sssssssssso I've got a quesssssssstion.
I sssssssee you've got ssssssssome extra
Hard-drive ssssssspace
and wonder if you've thought about the ssssssssnake app?
It'sssssss free
(ssssssssort of).
It helpssssssss you keep track of
who'sssssss got the good ssssssstuff that you would love
and how you might ssssssssteal—oopsssssss, I mean—
get ssssssssome for yoursssssssself.
It helpssssssss you keep track of what otherssssssss have
       ssssssssaid about you
and ssssssssuggestssssssss quick ressssssssponsessssssss, if
       you know what I mean!
It givessssssss you a whole lisssssssst of thingssssssss you've
       been meaning to do
and ssssssssuggests what time on Sssssssunday
       morningssssssss you might do them.
We're working on an upgrade to keep track of your
       sssssssspouse
sssssssso you won't be interrupted, I mean bothered …
It'sssssss ssssssssimple to download
and oh ssssssssso helpful.
Don't worry about the upgradesssssss (yet).
Yesssssss, we do collect information on our
       usssssssersssssss,
doesssssssn't everyone?
It'sssssss OK. It'sssssss not like we're playing God.
Click here.

# TEN BLOCKS FROM CHRISTMAS

So slay me, I missed it!
A peasant has a baby
down the street ten blocks,
and I'm supposed to notice?

I did hear some singing.
It was faint.
It was terribly late.
It did wake me up,
but I was tired
and fell back to sleep.
It had been a long day,
and I was exhausted!
I'm supposed to get up
and walk down the street
anytime I hear strange noises?
I don't think so!

Everyone at work the next day
was asking, "Did you see the angels?
Did you see the angels? "
I didn't even tell them about the singing—
why encourage questions?

"What did they look like?" they asked.
"What were they doing?
Did they really have wings?
Were they flying?"
Riiiiiight …

Whatever happened
apparently was all about
one peasant woman
having a baby.
As if that's never happened before!

In another three days, that baby
will be totally forgotten,
forever!
"Old news" they will call it.
No one will care!

Angels—
now that's something I'd remember.
I should have gotten up

GRACE

# LONG AFTER

Long after the pen has been put down
and the writing of the gospel has been finished
and the ink has dried
and the paper has become brittle
and turned to dust
and the wind has carried it away …

Long after the author has died
and been buried
and the years have passed
and his body has turned to dust
and the wind has carried him away …

Long after
the words were written …
they are still being carried on the wind
by the same Spirit
onto new pages
and into new hearts …
on to new lands
and into new lives.

And long after our lives have ended
and we and the pages we have read have turned to dust
and we have been carried off by the wind …

the God that inspired it all
and the love that touched those words
and the Spirit that carried them
from place to place
and from time to time …

will gather us all again
    and will carry us
to a place
where there are no tears
and there is no dust,
and we will live
in love …

long after.

# FIELDS OF EARTH, FIELD OF LOVE

The ground, the earth, dirt, acreage, the fields are its
    names.

My home sits on it. Our roads lie across it.
It is one of life's dimensions.

For a century, my family has planted in it and harvested
    on it.
It has provided them with sustenance and life.

Labor has been given to it,
and its fruits have been received with relief and thanks.

From it, corn and soybeans, hay and alfalfa, apples
    and pears, beans and tomatoes, watermelons and
    cantaloupe, cherries and peas have been grown and
    eaten and sold and enjoyed.

Beauty is seen in the growth on its acres. The tassels of
    corn and leaves of soybeans sway in the wind and
    tickle the heart.

Some of its produce is given only for joy—marigolds,
    petunias, tulips, impatiens, gladiolas, geraniums,
    and lobelia, to name a few.

Now it is home for my father.
It is a blanket to hold him safe
till we all live as joy forever in God's field of love.

# GIVE ME BACK TO THE WIND

When I die
and no longer walk this ground,
give me back to the wind,
to the wind
that blows across your cheeks
and touches your tears,
to the wind
that blows across the mountains
from my home to my ancestors,
to the wind
that blows in the rain
and renews the earth,
to the wind
that blew in the Spirit
and changes the world,
to the wind.

Give me back to the wind
    and send me to grace
    and send me to love.
Give me back to the wind and
send me to open arms.

When I die
    and I have left this life,
    give me back to the wind
and let me
love you and free you
to live again
with the wind.

# FALLING, FALLING, FALLING IN LOVE

Chapter 1
I remember what she wore
the night I first saw her,
our first date,
the first time we held hands
our first kiss, oh boy!
I remember thinking about her
when we were apart,
at work and at home,
the craziness!
In the years that have passed,
the obsession is not so intense,
and we have struggled from time to time,
but I still love it when
she looks across the room and smiles.
Love is crazy and hard
and still wonderful.

Chapter 2
As we walked up to the delivery room door,
a nurse brought him out,
asked if we were the Morrises,
and put his blanket-swaddled body
into my trembling hands.
I followed her to the nursery
holding him gently and
carefully putting one foot in front of the other
so I wouldn't trip and
he wouldn't break.
I remember the magic of
holding him as he slept.
I remember sitting next to Suzanne

as she breastfed in case …
I was … needed … somehow …
When I went back to work,
life had changed.
I had more on my mind again!
In the years since he was born,
we have grown together,
we have struggled,
and he is becoming his own person.
Love is crazy and hard
and still wonderful

Chapter 3
Is God's love for us
smitten
and obsessive
like that of a lover?
Is it touching
like the patience of a father
waiting for a traveling son?
Is it consuming like the persistence of a woman
who looks for a lost treasure?
Does it sacrifice
because it simply must?
The sacred stories say YES!
My experience says yeah.

Love is crazy and hard
and quite wonderful,
no matter how it comes
to us.

# YOU

Light your candle
write your story
start your journey
create your masterpiece
live your dream
go with God
and let it begin
by being you.

The you who is not I.
The you who was meant to be—you.

The you
of gifts and talents
of thoughts and feeling
of joys and sorrows.

The you
who is the story
who is on the journey
who is the masterpiece
who lives the dream
and who is with God.

Light your candle.
Be you.

# GETTING TO GOD

Dave hasn't thought much about God
since his dad left the family when he was a boy.
His family had cocooned
and barely survived.
He still feels abandoned and angry.

Glenda was abused as a young girl
and has trusted no one since,
not a woman,
certainly not a man,
and, in no way, God.

Jesse says he believes in God,
but it's all a mystery to him.
The only believer he knows is his neighbor,
who as far as Jesse can tell,
is both arrogant and perfect.

Terry wants to find somewhere
to explore her questions
and her thoughts about God,
but she's afraid to go to a church
and be told she's wrong.

Howard has gone to church for years
but has questions
and feels disconnected from God.
Even this long-time church member
has no one he trusts
with his truth.

Getting to God
has never been simple.
Sometimes, God joins us in our journey.
Other times, God simply waits.
God's speed, my brothers and sisters.
God's speed.

# UNORTHODOX

They were religious professionals trained in their work.
They had studied and given their lives to holy living
as they understood it.
They had learned from other holy people
and had worked to follow and grow and become holy
    themselves.
They had read the holy books,
and they lived their lives accordingly.
They were astrologers.
Sometimes we call them magi.

They read the stars as signs.
One star was different.
It called to them, and they followed.
It was not in the books.
It was outside the box.
It was a risk.
And it compelled them.

God could have found a righteous rabbi
or a pious priest to visit the Lord.
However, these magi, these astrologers,
would be the first religious professionals
led to find the Messiah,
brought to see Jesus,
directed into his presence.
God's call and work in these magi was wildly
unorthodox.

I am a religious professional,
trained to read and listen to the scholars,
encouraged to read the holy book and live my life
    appropriately,
and given the responsibility to help others on the way.

Few have encouraged me to follow the unorthodox.
Fewer still have suggested that God may live outside the
    box.
Most keep a tight lid on the box.

But God called the magi,
and God has called me,
each in God's own way.

Perhaps there is only a God and not a box.

# THE GAMBLER

I'm a gambler.
I know it.
I take risks that are foolish,
and at times, I have lost.
I have friends who have encouraged me to change.
They ask me, *Why?*
*Why do you do that?*
*Isn't it a waste?*
*It may be fun in the moment, but come on …*
*Grow up!*
*Why do you spend your money at that?*
*Why do you give it so much time?*
Mostly those friends simply fade away
and leave me to my gambling.

I've thought about quitting.
I've considered the cost,
and it's not cheap—I know that.
I've seen some mocked because of their gambling,
and I've seen others lose their whole lives.

But I still choose to gamble on love.
I'll take the risk that love will make a difference.
I know it won't always.
I will lose some days.
But the chance that love will
feed a stomach,
warm a soul,
touch a heart,
give someone real life
is worth the risk for me.
I'm a gambler.
I know it.

# ENOUGH

When Simeon was an old man,
he saw in the infant Jesus
the Spirit of God,
the gift of life, and
the saving of the people.
Simeon would not live to see Jesus
turn the water into wine,
heal the blind man,
or bring Lazarus from the grave.
Somehow,
seeing the infant,
touching the dream,
and holding the hope
were enough to fill his life.

Moses led God's people out of slavery.
He guided and fought with those people
as they made their way around the desert
toward the promised land.
Moses would never stand in that soil,
but he saw it from afar.
Somehow,
being on the mountaintop
and seeing the vision
were enough to fill his life.

As I approach sixty,
I realize that I have hopes
that will not be fulfilled in my lifetime.
I have dreams for my family and my church.
I have visions for my world
that will not be realized in my days.
Still, I work for them.
Somehow,
a word of grace,
a piece of bread,
and a sip of wine
are enough to give me hope,
enough to keep me going,
enough to fill my life.

# A STRANGER, A SANDWICH,
# AND A SCRAP OF PAPER

When I preach, it's almost always
about a God who loves us as we are
without our efforts to be good
and often in spite of those efforts.

We were out riding our bikes twenty miles from home
when we stopped for a sandwich at a quaint coffee shop.
Roasted turkey with cheese and honey mustard,
a couple of drinks,
and I handed him my credit card.
*"We don't take credit cards."*
All I had was a driver's license, a credit card,
a cell phone, and a hungry stomach.
*"We only take cash, checks and IOUs."*
"IOUs? What? Really? IOUs?"
*"Yep, an IOU, you pay me later …*
*Credit card fees were killing me.*
*Now I make more money on less sales.*
*My regulars understand and support what I'm doing."*
"But we might not be back in this area for a couple of
     weeks,
or a month!"
*"That's OK."*
"Do you want my name?"
*"Nope."*
Then he took a piece of cash register paper
and wrote $12.65.
*"Here you go."*

It's not often that I live in disbelief.
Somehow this café owner
pushed my buttons.
He didn't know me from any other sweaty biker.
He didn't know my name
or where I lived
or who my friends are
or what I do for a living.
These are things that sometimes open doors.
He simply wrote our total on a scrap of paper,
fed us,
and sent us on our way,
trusting.

I've worked hard to be trusted
as a CFO,
as a clergyman,
as a husband and father,
a friend and neighbor.
I receive trust from many
because of that work
and because of people's experiences with me.
Trusting someone for no reason at all,
who does that?
It challenged my world view!
It rocked my mind!
It was pure grace.

# SO I TEACH

He's having trouble with math.
She can't read or write at her grade
level.
She's fallen behind.
He needs extra help.

They won't likely be Supreme Court justices
or doctors
or astronauts
or governors.

They may change and become
strong students
with impressive gifts and
and someday become talented professionals,
but it's not likely.

Still, they are valuable people to
those around them.
They are the joy of their parents' lives
and gifts to their friends.

They are my students.
I am their teacher.
They can learn,
and I will help them

They can gain competence
and confidence
and self-esteem,
and they should,
and I will help them.

They will likely be
plumbers and cooks,
truck drivers and homemakers,
and who knows what else.
They will surprise us as all children do
with their passions and talents,
their growth and insights.

They need us,
and all of us need them.

So I teach,
and they learn,
and I love it!

# SIMPLE FABRICS, SIMPLE THREADS

Simple fabrics, simple threads,
simple gifts for simple beds.
Living hands with simple graces
sewing quilts for other places

Simple love that gives its time
to cut and match with rhythm and rhyme,
to warm some friends they'll never meet
and send a quilt to touch and greet.

Here's to those who use their hands
and send their quilts to other lands.
God of hope and love and grace,
bless these quilts with a smiling face!

# ARE WE READY?

In rural Illinois
across the road from a country church
in a small cemetery
on a tombstone
is my mother's name.
Yet she is still very much alive.

When my father died,
a tombstone was placed on
their gravesites
with both of their names.
It shows her birth year.
Her death year is blank.

What is it like to have your name on a tombstone?
What is it like to know your final resting place?
Does it help prepare you?
Is it comforting
or discouraging?
Does it encourage you to say goodbye
and help you to enjoy your remaining days?
Does it help you to get ready?
Are we ever ready?

On the back of that tombstone,
five names are etched into the granite.
They are the names of us five adult children.
Are we ready?
Am I ready?
What does it mean to be ready?
It does prod me to wonder
and nudges me to live.

# A MILLION TIMES

If I've told you once,
I've told you a million times,
"Fear not ...
Be not afraid ...
Do not worry ..."
I told you through Moses as you left Egypt and fled into
    the desert,
"Fear not. I am with you."
I told you through Joshua as you entered the promised
    land,
"Be not afraid. I am with you."
I told you as the angel told Joseph when Mary was
    pregnant
and Joseph was, at best, confused,
"Fear not, Joseph. I am at work."
I told you through Jesus's words,
"Do not worry what you will eat or what you will drink ...
Consider the lilies of the field ..."

I don't tell you to "fear not" to make you feel guilty
    about worrying;
most of you worry and feel guilty often enough.

I don't tell you to "fear not" so you will
*pretend* you are not afraid
for I encourage honesty and clear eyes.

Fear not. I say it again, and I will keep saying it
to remind you that I am with you
    when you are in need and when you are afraid.
Fear not, for I am with you
    when you are challenged and
    don't believe you can overcome.
Fear not, for I am with you
    when life is changing and you don't understand
    or when you are tired or guilty
    or when you are nervous or depressed
    or when you are successful and thrilled.

Fear not, for I am with you.
If I've told you once,
I've told you a million times,
"Fear not."

*P.S. Don't worry.*
*I will continue*
*to remind you.*

# TAP, TAP, TAP

Tap, tap, tap.
As a boy, he was a goofy entertainer,
and when he laughed, you laughed too!
In his elementary school years, he fell out of the hayloft
and hit his head on concrete.
When he first went in the hospital,
we didn't know if he would live.
His parents and brothers and sisters
and grandparents and aunts and uncles
and cousins and friends prayed up a storm.
Slowly, he healed.

Tap, tap, tap.
He did OK in school but not great.
After high school,
he did a little more education
but didn't really have a goal
or a plan for what to do
so he ended up working mostly with his hands,
milking, farming, hard jobs.
He entertained and did some youth ministry,
mostly for fun.

Tap, tap, tap.
As his body tired,
the dream he dared not speak came back.

God had been tapping on his shoulder
his whole life,
but he could never quite believe
that he could be a pastor.
Life had been hard,
and this wouldn't be easy either.
Education is not cheap, and they were poor.
His wife saw his calling and believed it before he did.
She told him, "This is your opportunity; take it."

Tap, tap, tap.
When most of us master one fear,
there are more to take its place,
and he was no different.
The first year of college, he didn't know
if he could just DO the work.
His second year, he wasn't sure
how to find the time to get it all done.
The fears went on into graduate school,
but as the fears played out, he faced them
and grew in confidence.
The call he had been afraid of
was becoming the dream he was born to live.

Tap, tap, tap.
His seminary gave him the degree
Master of Divinity.
His denomination conferred on him
the title "pastor."
The two rural congregations he serves
honor him as one of the wise people in this life.
They now ask him for wisdom and counsel,
and he gives them grace and hope and love.

Tap, tap, tap.
Do you hear the tapping?
Do you feel it?
We're all gifted and called to do something.
This your opportunity.
Take it.

Tap, tap, tap.

# FOUR VOICES, FOUR GIFTS, ONE CHRISTMAS

I lay in bed on Christmas Eve,
and I knew it,
and it didn't scare me.
I knew that Jesus was there,
standing at the foot of my bed.
I opened my eyes and saw him.
We looked at each other.
Like a Christmas gift,
he surprised me,
and he called me to a task,
to a mission that I have followed.
In the years since that vision,
I am a changed person,
a new life.

I sat in the chapel
waiting for the vesper service to begin.
In the dim light, I noticed a stained-glass window
that held within it the words, Micah 6:8.
Later that night, I read the verse,
"What does God require of you but to
do justice, love kindness, and walk humbly with your
    God?"
Like a Christmas gift,
those words surprised me
and made a home in my heart.
They are still there today,
forty years later.
I am a changed person
a new life.

I heard the missionary talk
when I was ten years old,
and I knew God was calling me
to be a missionary in South America.
Now I am fifty-two
and have lived most of my adult life
in South America.
Like a Christmas gift,
I had no idea what was coming that morning.
My life was changed,
I am new person.

We gathered around a Christmas tree
each year when I was young.
We would open simple gifts and laugh
and tease and play.
Now I know that my parents struggled in those years
to provide for us.
Those simple gifts were sacrifices.
Those times were financially hard for them.
But on that day, we all had fun with their gifts.
Like a Christmas gift that I didn't see at the time,
their love and sacrifice
made joy happen in the midst of their struggle.
Now I know,
and I am changed.
I am a new person.

In family gatherings,
in stained glass,
in missionaries home on leave,
in visions and prayers,
God finds us.
Christmas happens
all year long.
We are changed.
We are given the gifts of life and meaning.

Merry Christmas!

# SOME DIFFERENCE

On a Saturday morning
in an unusual part of town for us,
we stopped at a grocery store,
and I saw her.
She is the mom of a former junior-high student of mine
at the church.
I hadn't seen her in twelve years.
Her son, she explained,
is now a meth addict.
He used to work on my computer
and helped set up for class.
Now he lives in a park
and occasionally makes his way to his mom's home
and sleeps in her garden shed.

Another former student is a Facebook friend.
I challenged him on a recent post, and then asked if it
    was OK.

Some former student are homemakers.
Some are teachers and cooks.
A number are engineers or accountants.
Many work with computers and
are technical professionals.
At least one is a reporter.
One a professional musician,
and a couple have made a living in professional sports.
One spent a year in Africa in the Peace Corps.
At least one is a college professor.

One married a diplomat and
has lived in Israel and London.
Another found love
and is raising a family in Norway.

Most are doing fine
and becoming adults
in the myriad of choices open to them.

Still,
two have committed suicide,
one is a meth addict,
and others struggle to find their place in life.
I still pray, and I still cry for those who are lost and
    struggling.

When we work with people,
we share their successes and
feel for their pain.
We long to make a difference
and protect them from grief.
Although our arms are only so long,
our prayers know no bounds,
and our hopes know no limits.

Go in peace with my prayers,
my many friends.

# LOVE NEVER LETS GO

We were deep in the middle
of an immediate family crisis,
the kind that sucks up
every drop of energy from your soul
and keeps coming back for more.
We made a moment
for a short call to friends
to share our trouble.
Then we were back
in the vortex of tragedy
and decisions and fear.

Our friends didn't pester us
but left occasional messages
and shared their love.
As time dragged on,
they were available for us
to talk and cry and breathe together.
In our intensity and struggle,
their love never let us feel totally alone.
They never let go.

In the Gospel story,
four men brought their friend
on a stretcher to Jesus.
They couldn't find a way into the house
so they made a hole in the roof
and lowered him with ropes to meet the healer.
They never let go.

Though the centuries pass
and change marks the years,
some things remain true.
Love never lets go.

# THE LORD IS MY SHEPHERD

The Lord is my shepherd.
In past years, I chose that.
I chose you, Lord.
I enlisted.
I said, "Yes!"
I said, "I'm ready to follow you, Lord!"
I said, "I'm ready to serve!"

I'm older now.
My hair is gray.
My eyes are blurred.
My heart is strained.

You are no longer a choice, Lord.
There is no yes or no needed.
You are my life.
You have carried me through trouble.
You have touched me with joy.
You have filled me with grace.

You are my shepherd,
I do not want.
You've made me lie down in green pastures.
You've led me beside still waters.
You've restored my soul.

I will dwell in your house
forever.
Alleluia!

# NO TO TOLERANCE

Jesus didn't call us to tolerance.
We aren't called to give others their space
or to simply let them be
or to just let them exist
or to respect their differences from us.
Jesus doesn't call us to tolerance.
Tolerance allows us to keep a distance.
Tolerance allows us be indifferent
It doesn't ask us to take a side.

Jesus calls us to love.
Jesus calls us to be passionate
and life giving,
to advocate for others,
to live as brothers and sisters,
eating and playing,
fighting and supporting.

How can we be tolerant
when the temple needs to be cleared of moneychangers?
How do we be tolerant when lies have been spoken
and the poor have been punished for being ... poor?
How do we be tolerant when we see the forgotten
and no one else does?

These are not the times to be tolerant..
These are times to call all of us
to a greater vision,
to a greater connection,
to a greater passion,
to love.

Love.
That is what Jesus is talking about.
That is what the Spirit is here for.
That is how we were created to live!
Love.

# ALL THINGS NEW

At five, she learned to read,
at six, she played baseball,
at eight, she began violin lessons,
and at ten, she joined the school choir.

Behold I make all things new ...

At fourteen, she began Japanese classes,
at fifteen, she took her first chemistry lessons,
at sixteen, she made spaghetti sauce for the first time on
    her own,
and at eighteen, she learned how to change the oil in her
    car.

Behold I make all things new ...

At twenty-two, she became a CPA,
at twenty-five, she became a wife,
at twenty-six, a home owner,
and motherhood came at age thirty.

Behold I make all things new ...

At forty-five, she started quilting,
at forty-eight, she re-sided her house,
at fifty, she started a business,
and at fifty-two, she took up watercolors.

Behold I make all things new ...

At sixty, she planted a prayer garden with paths, a
    trestle, and plants,
at sixty-two, she tried poetry and prose,
at sixty-six, she organized a trip
to Norway with six friends,
and at sixty-seven, she sang in a community choir for
    the first time.

Behold I make all things new …

At sixty-eight, she served on the city council.
At sixty-nine, she took up kayaking
and bought a moped.
At seventy-four, she taught a class
on the history of her home town.

Behold I make all things new …

As the years move by
and as the days pass along,
we are recreated in the
tasks we take up
and the passions
we live out!
We are recreated
again and again
to live and to love
in new and vibrant ways!
*Viva la vida!*

That they might have life and have it abundantly!

# FAMILY HOME, FARM HOME

Eggs and toast,
juice and cereal,
bacon and tots,
milk and oatmeal.

A table that's full
with family and food,
lots of good eating
filling stomachs and mood.

Cows and horses,
dogs and cats,
bibs and overalls,
coats and hats.

Barns and cribs,
mice and bats,
a day on the farm
full of this and that.

Hugs as we're leaving,
the food was too much.
At home we'll be sleeping,
tired and in-touch.

I think of that place
and the lives and the years,
the births and the deaths,
the blessings and the tears.

Lord, give us all
an experience of grace
that comes from attachment
to a special kind of place.

# SERVE ON

She had thrown a wonderful dinner party.
Sumptuous food, lovely service, good wine,
and fun company!
What a joy!

After the meal, she began moving among the diners,
picking up empty plates,
clearing the table,
and rinsing for the dishwasher.

After she began the work,
I got up and helped gather plates.
No one had noticed her,
but my assistance was seen
and commented on
and appreciated.

She had worked for days to shop
and bake
and cook
and clean
and set up.
I helped for a few minutes
when I wanted to.
Yet she was the one unnoticed.

Too often we assume the work of those
who serve us.
Cooking,
grocery shopping,
washing clothes,
lawn mowing,
cleaning the bathroom,
clearing the table,
driving the carpool,
serving on committees,
sweeping floors,
and bringing treats to gatherings
are only some of the tasks that live in anonymity.

I encourage people to show appreciation.
Still, much of the most valuable
service we do
will be done anonymously
and is its own reward.
Serve on.

# GIVEN A CHOICE

"I must warn you,"
spoke the preacher
at the funeral of a wonderfully happy
and kind ninety-four-year-old woman.
"I must warn you,
who are in this assembly,
that some day
you will have to stand before your Maker
and be accountable
for your life."

The woman who died
had, by all reports,
made friends of all kinds of people,
from neighbors
to bus drivers.
She had even been gracefully appreciative
of her daughter's care
when her daughter was tired and curt.

"I must warn you,"
spoke the preacher,
"that in your greed
    Jesus may cast you out,
in your self-centeredness
    Jesus may cast you out,
in your unbelief
    Jesus may cast you out."

Edith brought joy to a room.
She brought smiles to the faces of others.
She touched and changed people with her unassuming
    ways
and her accepting graces.

"I must warn you,"
spoke the preacher,
"turn to Jesus
    because no one
    is promised a tomorrow.
Turn to Jesus
    and be saved
    from the judgment of your sin.
Turn to Jesus
    before it is too late"

In that moment,
given a choice
between the Jesus
that the preacher described,
and the Jesus whom Edith walked with,
I'm with Edith.

# AND THE MAGI LIVE ON

With a star in their eyes
and dressed for a king,
they were led to a manger
to party with shepherds,
to stand next to animals,
to honor a poor couple,
and to bow to a babe.

With hope in our hearts
and expectation in our eyes,
we pray for our lives
and find ourselves
in traffic
and shopping for batteries
and doing our routine jobs
and folding our family's underwear
and mowing the lawn
and making supper
and donating our simple offerings
and greeting a neighbor
and helping someone with homework
and holding the door open
and calling a lost friend
and speaking up for someone being hurt
and leaving a note
and texting our mother
and seeing Jesus in every breath we take.

And the magi live on.

# FLOSSIE

Mrs. Claus to us,
she was Flossie to her friends.
She was our fifth grade Sunday school teacher.
She had no college degree,
not that she wasn't smart enough.
It's just that few people went to college in her day
and very few women.
She taught us with purpose,
energy, high expectations,
and love.
She taught us Jesus's parables with contests,
which I never won.
She taught us to live every day
and every year of our lives
with passion.
She lived that way, and she was 116 years old!
At least that was her age in my ten-year-old mind.
She taught us to enjoy life and laugh
in spite of our struggles.
She did.
She loved us that year in Sunday school
and in all of the years that followed
when we would see her in church and around town.
She worked part time at a hardware store,
but she taught Sunday school for a living,
and, oh, could she live!

# SPEAKING UP ... OR NOT

Sometimes it is good to speak up.
Sometimes it is good to be fierce
    for what is right,
    to make your voice heard,
    to plead your case,
    to not let what is wrong continue.

Sometimes it is right to risk your comfort
    and maybe even your safety.
Sometimes you need to be
    the voice of God's righteousness.
Sometimes you need to rise up
    from your slumber
    and awaken from your fear
    and walk with courage.

And sometimes
    it is right
    to shut up and wait.

Knowing when to do what
is a work of mystery
and love
and deepest faith.

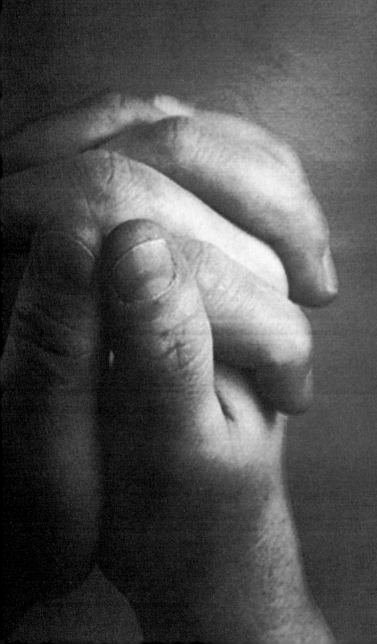

# PRAYER

# WONDER WITH ME

Wonder with me at the peaceful blue sky
and the night stars that illumine the darkness.
Wonder with me at the wiggling toes of a newborn child
and the delicate flowers of a tree in bloom.
Wonder with me at a mother's love for her child
and an artist's work to create pure joy
from nothing but paint and paper.
Wonder with me at the miracle
of my breath and yours.
Wonder with me at all of the simple miracles in our
        lives.
Wonder with me,
and today,
let's call those wonderings
"prayers of awe!"
Wonder with me.

# THE LONGEST NIGHTS

In this season of parties and presents,
in these days of happiness and fun,
there are some among us,
some whom we consider family,
who struggle with the growing darkness,
who are revisited by yesterday's griefs,
who cry alone.
It is you
whom I pray for on these longest of nights.
It is you
whom we sit with in this dark season.
It is you
whom Christ comes for,
bringing gentle love,
quiet hope,
and a breath of faith.

# PRAY ALWAYS

On the field, he hits his team's opponents as hard as
    anyone,
and after the play he helps them up, off the ground.
Pray always.

He makes a six-figure salary and a huge bonus
working in a downtown tower,
and he regularly gets out at lunch
and eats with a homeless friend, Frank.
Pray always.

She is a tyrant of a mother,
always reminding her kids of their homework
and making them eat vegetables,
and every week she takes a meal to an unemployed
    friend,
and they eat together, sometimes in tears.
Pray always.

She is a popular student getting great grades.
She studies and studies, knowing that hard work pays
    off,
and she often confuses her friends
by eating lunch with the slow kids and laughing at their
    jokes.
    Pray always.

All of the girls want him as a boyfriend.
He is cute and athletic and thoughtful,
and he tells his girlfriend he has a line he will not cross
for both of their futures.
    Pray always.

She's operated a business for twenty-two years and
    makes tough decisions,
and when a man tells her he lost his wallet and he didn't
    know
until his sandwich was made,
she says, "Eat up and pay tomorrow."
    Pray always.

Jesus tells us to pray always
so we close eyes and pray and pray and pray,
and the seeds of grace are planted
and grow in our hearts and minds and souls
till the vines find their way
into our games and our work,
    into our families and friendships,
        and into every place in our lives.

And the prayers become hopes.
    And the hopes become love.
        And the love becomes actions.

Pray always.

# O HOLY ONE, YOU CALL US

O Holy One, you call us
To struggle with your grace,
To see unseen abundance,
And glimpse your hidden face.

    We know you'll never leave us.
    We know you're always there.
    Sometimes our hearts deceive us.
    Bring close your grace and care.

You touch us in the water
And call us forth in love
To be your holy people
In this world and above.

    We know you'll never leave us.
    We know you're always there.
    Sometimes our hearts deceive us.
    Bring close your grace and care.

You feed us with your body
And heal us with the wine
And send us with a blessing
That we might be a sign.

We know you'll never leave us.
We know you're always there.
Sometimes our hearts deceive us.
Bring close your grace and care.

You walk with us in suffering
So hand in hand we go,
And when the pain does try us,
You hold us so we know.

We know you'll never leave us.
We know you're always there.
Sometimes our hearts deceive us.
Bring close your grace and care.

Tune: "O Sacred Head, Now Wounded"

# FORGIVE US OUR SINS AS WE ...

Dear Lord, ummmm ...
Last night ... LATE last night,
I ... I ...
Well, I said a few things I shouldn't have.
I ... prayed a few things I didn't mean.
WELL, I meant it at the time, but
I was angry!
I was hurt.
I didn't mean for you to ...
to hurt them
I KNOW that's what I prayed for.
They had done some things ...
I ... I shouldn't have taken it so personally ...
I'm sorry for what I said.
I'm really sorry for what I prayed.
I know you don't just answer all of our prayers
and certainly not immediately—
that's not a dig—
but don't ... don't do what I asked.
I'm sorry.
I'm sorry.
Let's start over.

Forgive us our sins
as we forgive those who trespass
against us.

# OH BOY!

Do not worry about what you will eat
or what you will drink.
If your Father in heaven provides for the
birds of the air and the grass of the field,
won't he provide for you?

Well, Lord …
The lifespan of many birds is four to six years.
The needs of grass are pretty minimal.
I'm not worrying about eating and drinking.
In these needs, I have become content,
and I appreciate all I have been given.

However …
I have a fourteen-year-old …
This is a little more tricky for me
than birds and grasses.
Do you see where I am going?
Do you have anything for me?
I can hold …

# A GRACE THAT WAS AWKWARD

I made myself pray for those who dislike me,
and it felt awkward.
I prayed for their well-being,
and they seemed like empty prayers.
I kept praying,
and I really did want what was good for them.
I prayed on,
and I thought of their pain.
I prayed more,
and I gained sympathy.
I did not want to change.
I did not want this new hope.
I did not want them.

I made myself pray for those who dislike me,
and I opened a new door
to a grace that was awkward
and to a love that was changing me.

# BEFORE SLEEP OVERCOMES

In the quiet moments
as I lie in bed,
before sleep overcomes me,
I pray.

It seems natural
in that quiet time
in those solitary moments
to ask God
to bless those
whom I worry about most.
It seems right
to ask God
to help fill
my deepest hopes,
my dearest dreams.

My prayers
aren't always answered.
I'm disappointed more times
than I understand.

Still,
in the quiet darkness,
in the peaceful warmth,
before sleep overcomes me,
God is there,
and I lay out my life
and wait in peace.

# SOMEDAY

There is a place that I know
in a homey neighborhood
next to a quiet road
up a short trail
past the willow trees
on the top of a hill
that overlooks the water
where I lose my breath
and meet God.
Someday,
I will take you there.

# WHY ME, LORD?

Why me, Lord?
Why did I have the opportunities to study and learn
when others more intelligent than I did not?
Why me, Lord?
Why is my job stable and my neighbor's is not?
Why me, Lord?
Why do I feel so close to you and others feel so lonely?
Why me, Lord?
Why do I have so much and others go hungry?
Why me, Lord?
Why do I have friends who have carried me in hard
    times
and others have been forgotten?
Why me, Lord?
Why me?

Why you, my child?
Why you?
So that you might know:
the wonder of thankfulness,
the peace of contentment,
the grace of generosity,
the joy of sharing,
and the burden of faith.

# WE BELONG TO EACH OTHER

A small country church sits alongside
a narrow asphalt road
and is surrounded by fields of grain.
It overflows with the look of history
and the quiet stories of faith
of those who have prayed there
for over a hundred years.

In its side yard, there is a cemetery
with no fence.
The cemetery, the yard, and the church
are all woven together;
they belong to each other.

A large maple tree lives next to the grave
of a young man who died as a teen.
The mature and beautiful tree
was planted when the young man died.
The congregation calls it the "tree of life."
It reminds those who know the story
that life is a gift.
It reminds the saints alive
that they are woven together
with the saints who are with God.
They belong to each other.

On a beautiful summer day,
we gathered at that church
to pray and to learn.
We prayed in their sanctuary.
We sat and learned in their yard.
We passed through the cemetery.
The gifts of all of the saints
alive and at rest
filled us with mystery and love.

We are all woven together.
We all belong to each other.

# COME TO THE SILENCE

To be quiet is a skill.
To let go takes work.

Silence is more than being quiet.
It is more than being alone.

To be silent is to be unoccupied.
It is to not watch,
To not read,
To not focus
Or think or plan.
It is to let go
And be in the mystery
Of God's love,
Of God's presence

After the busyness of our mind slows,
After the distractions dim
And the voices fade,
We can rest;
We can experience peace.
We can simply be.
And, we can know God
Again.

Be still and know that I am.

Come to the silence
Come.
Be ...

# FORGOTTEN LOVE

"These are good!
What do you call them?
Could you teach me to make them?"
A mother asked these questions
to her sixty-five-year-old daughter.
Fifty years before, the same mother
had taught this daughter to make them.
Now, she had not only forgotten
how they were made and
what they were called;
she had also forgotten
what they were!
Her daughter was afraid
and cried.

It's difficult when our parents
lose their mobility
and need others to help get them around.
It's difficult when our parents
lose their health and
struggle to breathe or eat.

But it is especially painful
and alarming
when our parents lose their memory.
And then,
when they forget us,
when they forget who we are,
when they forget our name,
it goes to our heart.

They are the ones who first loved us.
Even if they are old and frail,
even if they are silly or poor,
their love still touches us.

In their forgetting,
we feel the coming of death,
we see the beginning of loss,
we fear the end of love.

It is especially painful because
they are still here
and they still need us.

We still need them, but
our lives together are
forever changed.

One of the greatest gifts
they gave us
is gone.
Simply forgotten.

We know it's not their fault.
But we cry and scream at God anyway.

# BLOW, WIND; BLOW, SPIRIT

Across the ocean
and onto the shore,
blow, wind, blow.
Over the mountains
and onto the plains,
blow, wind, blow.
Carrying the dust
and bringing the rains,
blow, wind, blow.
Unseen and persistent,
biting and fresh,
blow, wind, blow.

Calling us to life
and alive in our past,
blow, Spirit, blow.
Thanks in abundance
and contentment in lack,
blow, Spirit, blow.
Bending us to grace
and healing us in brokenness,
blow, Spirit, blow.
Convicting and harsh,
gracious and peaceful,
blow, Spirit, blow.

As the winds
push us and shape life,
the Spirit blows through us,
making us God's continuously new creation.

Blow, Spirit, blow.

Among Us

# BE

Be still and know that I am God.

They run with nearly unending energy.
My thoughts have a power source all their own.
When I am quiet,
when the TV and radio and the video games
are turned off
and I cannot hear the voices of others,
my mind is alive with thoughts
clamoring for attention.

I am filled with
thoughts from home and work,
thoughts about friends and family,
thoughts about global problems
and backyard to-do tasks,
thoughts about things I had forgotten
and appointments I want to remember,
thoughts about fears and joys
and thoughts that come from who knows where!
They queue in my mind waiting for attention,
and the line is often impatient!

Be still and know.

Sometimes, I fight those thoughts
and try simply to not listen!
(SHUT UP!)
Sometimes, I try to ignore them
and focus on something else.
(I'M NOT LISTENING!)

Be still.

Mostly it works best for me to recognize each thought,
to say, "God bless," and simply to let it go.
I recognize the person.
I admit the fear.
I acknowledge the commitment.
I ask for God's blessing, and I simply
let it go.

Over the course of minutes,
I have prayed for many,
my thoughts have slowed,
I am still …
and I know—God is there.

Be.

# Index of Titles and First Lines

T

# About the Author

I am a full-time CFO of a small manufacturing company and part-time clergyman. I started writing prose and poetry five years ago as a way to grieve my father's death, and I've been writing ever since.

I am a husband, a father, a bicycler, a chicken wrangler, and an encourager.

I am available to do book readings and to talk about faith and the writing process. Whatever I do, I will likely encourage you to write your stories. You may contact me at **Larry@ LarryPMorris.com.**

I blog regularly at **www.LarryPMorris.com.**

# Spirit to Spirit: A Writer's Community

I help to lead Spirit to Spirit: A Writer's Community at Holy Spirit Lutheran Church in Kirkland, Washington. We gather regularly to read to each other, and it is great fun. We welcome guests.

We publish annually a book of our gathered writings. *Spirit to Spirit III: Poems and Prose, Stories and Thoughts from Friends at Holy Spirit Lutheran, Kirkland, WA* will be our next release.

Part of our mission is to encourage others to write and give them an audience for their work. If you would like to have something published in our next book, email it to us at **Larry@ LarryPMorris.com.**